SOUTH MANOR, RUDDINGTON, NOTTS.

Albert Hindley's Postcard Legacy

During the Golden Age of picture postcards (1902-18), Nottinghamshire was well-served by plenty of postcard publishers, both local and national. Some famous names from London - Blum & Degen, Rotary and Raphael Tuck - issued sets of Nottingham cards. The bulk of Edwardian city and county views, though, came from two independent operators based on Clumber and Pelham Streets. From the latter location came R. (Robert?) Henson, who was almost certainly responsible for the 'Peveril' series of postcards that covered the city fairly randomly during the Edwardian era. Operating from Clumber Street, though, was the redoubtable Albert Hindley, who published many hundreds of picture postcards covering Nottingham city, the suburbs, and outlying villages from late 1904 onwards, probably until 1908. The earliest card in the series that I've seen postally used is 4th January 1905. In the early 20th century, Hindley operated a music shop and printing business at 21 Clumber Street, though it had begun life under his stewardship as a fancy goods shop. The titles above his windows read 'Pianos, Organs, Violins' on one side, and 'Printer & Bookbinder' on the other. You'd assume Hindley might have printed his own postcards, though Grenville Jennings, an avid collector of the postcards, asserted that he was told by Albert's son Harold that the printing of the cards was outsourced to a Glasgow firm, Millar & Lang. Unusually for a local Edwardian postcard publisher, all Hindley's cards (styled the 'Clumber' series after the shop's street location) were coloured, the colour being hand-painted onto the original photos, most of which Albert Hindley took himself. All the cards are numbered, which make them much easier to catalogue and collect, although plenty of anomolies exist. They run to 658 at least - though, because there are apparent gaps from 400 onwards, the total number of postcards published might be around 400-450. The missing numbers were apparently used in a 'Peveril' series, probably published by Robert Henson, most of which are numbered in the 500s. Sometimes the suffix 'a' was added to the number, for no apparent reason. Sometimes the same number was used for different views, and a few cards carry no number at all. Largely, though, the sequence is straightforward. There's an interesting mix of churches, streets, canals, railway stations and architecture, the bulk of the cards being single pictures, though later Hindley experimented with multi-views, heraldic motifs and borders. Apart from occasional forays into Derbyshire and Leicestershire, all the scenes feature Nottingham, its suburbs, and an area within 20 miles of the city centre. Hindley wasn't the only one to publish coloured postcards of Nottingham - top London firm Raphael Tuck produced a few attractive sets - but no firm in the country came anywhere near the 'Clumber' output of coloured postcards for a partcular area. Another Nottingham publisher of interest in the early 20th century is R. Fleeman, whose postcards were in the 'Broad Marsh series'.

When Harold Hindley retired in the 1960s, the shop became a TV rentals business, and is now a branch of Levi's Jeans.

The idea for the book

When I bought a collection of picture postcards in early 2019, I was pleased to see a large number of Nottinghamshire cards in a series titled 'Clumber', originally published in the early 20th century during the reign of King Edward VII. I had been familiar with the attractive coloured postcards for many years, but the presence of so many gave me an idea for this book. I chose 125 cards with the idea of revisiting the locations and taking photos from the same spot that the photographer had used. It sounded simple in theory, but in practice proved a really challenging - but fun - task, which has taken myself, photographer Rob Inglis, and my wife Mary to some interesting places. Some of the postcard locations no longer exist in their Edwardian form, having been bulldozed into history. Other places were difficult to access, and many of the photographic spots were in the middle of now very busy roads. But over a period of some six weeks we netted the lot, chasing the weather and light, using detective work and sometimes best guesses to replicate the original pictures. We aimed with each photo to provide a reasonable and interesting comparison with the original postcard, but sometimes the direction and perspective of the photography had necessarily to be different. It is entirely possible that we've misread the odd location, but this book is our best shot at showing how a selection of places in Edwardian Nottinghamshire have been transformed into what they are today. We hope you enjoy the result, and that you in turn feel inspired to search out some of the featured places. The tram route is ideal for most of the Nottingham locations!

Edwardian Nottinghamshire

The period between 1901 and 1910 (the Edwardian era) was in retrospect a golden decade, the last period of peace before internal unrest in Britain - strikes, suffragettes and the Irish situation - and the horrors of the First World War. The country had enjoyed an unparalleled period of peace since 1815 (the exceptions of the Crimean and Boer Wars didn't touch most people's lives), living conditions were improving, and leisure possibilities were increasing for most people. It was the Golden Age of theatre, football, cricket, trams and the railways, and a great time to be alive. I hope the postcards in this book reflect that. It is sobering, though, to look at the images of children in the streets and wonder what became of them. Check the postcard of East Bridgford on page 94 - how many of those boys pictured would survive the war a decade later? Looking at these postcards, too, it's amazing to reflect that the people featured were the occupants and guardians of the county's city, towns and villages at the time. Our grandparents, great grandparents and great-great grandparents walked these streets, travelled those trams, visited those theatres. This book is a glimpse into a very different, but immensely fascinating, world.

The locations and subjects

It is difficult to detect a definite plan in Hindley's publishing output, and subjects seem to have been chosen fairly randomly. Assuming he numbered the cards in publication order, it was either a case of producing pictures he thought would sell well, or perhaps publishing particular views at the request of local retailers. In the case of Nottingham, were the postcards published for tourists or locals, or both? Despite a wide coverage of the city, Hindley ignored the Trip to Jerusalem, the Salutation and the Royal Children pubs, and failed to venture inside Victoria railway station. He covered the Arboretum profusely, though. In the suburbs and villages, he generally featured churches (85 in the series), often cemeteries (11), and sometimes railway stations, ferries and country houses. The choice of these latter was also random, though. All five of these institutions loomed large in the life of village communities in 1906. While railways took villagers to nearby towns and cities, ferries were the only way of crossing the River Trent outside of Nottingham and Newark. Hindley might well have covered Southwell and Newark, but these places had their own postcard publishers, which is probably why he left them alone.

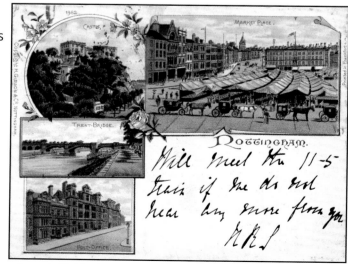

The importance of picture postcards at the time

The years 1902-18 are commonly known as the Golden Age of Picture Postcards, because of the phenomenal output from thousands of local and national publishers. Postcards became the email, text message and instagram of their day, a medium

An early Nottingham postcard from a German publisher, showing standard tourist views. This probably appeared in 1898 and was likely to appeal more to overseas visitors.

for writing a (normally) brief message and perhaps an excuse for not writing a long letter! They were also the go-to way of covering events and bringing the faces of popular personalities to the public at a time when newspaper photography was limited. The pictures on the cards featured everything under the sun - views of places, personalities from all walks of life, cartoons, numerous subjects (transport, politics, sport, fashion, religion, music) and appeared as almost miniature works of art or photography. Many tens of millions were posted each year, and people began to collect the postcards for their own sake, housing them in special albums. Many cards carried the message, *"here's another one for your collection"*.

The earliest picture postcards in the UK had appeared in 1894, when the Post Office allowed independent, private firms and individuals to publish postcards that could be sent through the mail using adhesive stamps. Cards were published but were not an immediate hit, generally being bought by tourists or businessmen from abroad and sent back overseas. At first the picture could only occupy a part of one side (restricting its impact), as the other was reserved exclusively for the address to where the postcard was being sent. In 1902, though, the Post Office allowed 'divided backs', where one side could be used for both message and address. From then the postcard craze really took off, and in the Edwardian era (until January 1910, when the King died) some six billion were sent through the post and countless billions more were bought to be kept in specially-manufactured albums. Postcards normally cost one halfpenny (the equivalent of £.002 now) and the required stamp the same amount. With the national average wage at the time thirty shillings (£1.50 in today's money), postcards were likely used (and collected) far more by the middle class. The high-water mark of the picture postcard's popularity was 1907, but the medium flourished until the end of the First World War in 1918. After that, rises in postage rates, a depressed national mood, and the increasing use of the telephone meant picture postcards gradually retreated to the comic and tourist view type.

Print runs and prices

It is impossible to know how many copies of each of Hindley's postcards were printed at the time. Using a commercial printer like Miller & Lang would probably mean a minimum run of at least 500 cards, and more viably 1,000. This would be fine for city locations, but would Papplewick residents, for example, have hoovered up that number very quickly? On some photos, Albert Hindley encouraged plenty of children to be part of the picture, but others featured totally empty streets. I have not been able to locate an M & L price list, but another Glasgow postcard printer quoted 19/6 (just under £1) for 500 hand-painted from photo cards and 29/- (£1.45) for 1,000. M & L may have been cheaper, but given that Hindley would have to wholesale the cards to shops, which probably sold them for one-halfpenny each, the profit margin doesn't seem great.

Main changes in the locations since 1904-8

Without a doubt the single biggest change from the first decade of the 20th century is the relentless presence of motorised transport today. So many of the 'Clumber' postcards showed children playing in the middle of what are now busy roads, or people ambling around without needing to avoid the traffic, or animals being herded down a street. Traffic then was the horse and cart, the odd bicycle, and, on some main routes, the recently-introduced electric tram. Motor cars were around, somewhere, in small numbers, but they are near-impossible to spot on Albert Hindley's postcards. Getting around in Nottinghamshire was less stressful and often quicker - at least in the city. In country villages, where many of the scenes have changed remarkably little, people's travel plans further than the distance of a decent walk would involve trains. Plenty of places had railway stations, even if sometimes they were inconveniently sited a mile or so away from the village centre.

The 115 years or so since the 'Clumber' postcards were published have seen major changes in Nottingham's architecture, not always for the better. Perhaps the clearest example of this is on Smithy (formerly Long) Row, but everywhere that has seen change can arguably be said to be less aesthetically pleasing. Of course, the demolition of slums and provision of better amenities makes life today so much more tolerable, but people in Nottingham in 1906 had an obvious thrill going to Goose Fair (in the Market Place) or seeing a production at the Theatre Royal. Messages on the back of picture postcards often refer to 'going out' in Nottingham. It is a shame, though, that the second half of the 20th century saw so much dismantling of great buildings, marvellous streets (think Drury Hill) and railway tracks. No-one in the 1960s apparently foresaw the potential of tourism - Drury Hill could have been Nottingham's very own Shambles - or the impact that traffic might have on the city. If all the tracks of closed railway lines had been left intact, there would have been countless arteries for trams to run on now.

And while we're on the subject of trams, a fascinating comparison of the two eras is made possible by the return of trams to Nottingham. Ubiquitous on Edwardian postcards, they are also a major presence in the city today. Few places in England have re-adopted this very green method of transport (I'm thinking Manchester, Sheffield and Birmingham), but Nottingham's forward-thinking City Council have been enthusiastic backers of trams since the turn of this century.

We've lost plenty of green spaces, of course, and suburban communities now merge seamlessly into each other. Clifton and Gamston villages have been overpowered by adjacent development, and the need for new housing has meant a relentless expansion of estates all over the area.

Where to find these postcards today

An amazing number of cards have survived through two world wars and generations of families, usually kept in special hard-wearing albums. Original Edwardian collections began to surface first in the 1960s and continued to come on the market for the next four decades. Now it is much rarer to find an original collection.

Today's collectors generally prefer photographic postcards that were produced using a developing process, but only small numbers could be produced this way (this, of course, makes such postcards rarer!). Any publisher wanting big sales would have to go down the printing route, either in black & white or colour. Most cards were published in monochrome, which makes Hindley's 'Clumber' series unusual and striking.

Edwardian postcards turn up in all kinds of places such as antique shops, car boot sales and specialist fairs (a very big postcard collectors' fair is held four times a year in Nottingham)*, and of course can be accessed on internet sites such as eBay.

Acknowledgments

Around half the photos in the book were taken by Rob Inglis, who I persuaded to do more walking than he's done for years, and who frequently put himself in danger by standing in the middle of roads to take photos. Rob's encyclopaedic knowledge of Nottingham streets helped us reach locations it would otherwise have taken me ages to find. The rest of the photos were taken by me, and I'd like to thank my wife Mary, who was on most of the trips and acted as chauffeur, researcher, and common sense adviser. Thanks, too, to the host of people we met on our trips who tried to point us in the right direction. Everyone was unfailingly polite, helpful and generally became engrossed in the project, though couldn't always find the answers! In Oxton, we involved a dozen people who tried to work out which pub had stood at Three Lane Ends - and even work out where Three Lane Ends had been! I complicated things here by suggesting we should be looking for the 'Old Oak' pub, located on Water Lane, but eventually we cracked it (see page 47). We were invited into a station house that has been turned into a railway museum and a residence full of meccano models, including a grandfather clock. We met residents of Woodthorpe Court who were proud to live on the site of a railway station, and at a golf clubhouse at Bulwell, bumped into a couple of council workers who couldn't stop talking about postcards and history, and insisted on taking me on a guided tour to the old Bulwell Hall stables. Unfortunately, they were out of bounds. We wondered how much trespassing to do to find the correct place to take photos, but most of all the three of us had a lot of fun doing this project. Hopefully you'll have as much pleasure exploring the results. Thanks also to my younger daughter Sandy Drummond, who advised on layout and helped greatly with publicity, to Marion Church for loaning some postcards and helping with the checklist, to Lesley Shuttleworth from Cropwell Bishop, and to Alan Morrison, who proof-read the book.

Brian Lund
June 2019

Where population figures are quoted in the text, these are taken from the 1901 and 2011 censuses respectively.

* King's Meadow Campus, Lenton Lane, Nottingham. Details 0115 937 4079 or www.postcardcollecting.co.uk

Nottingham Market Place

In Edwardian days, Nottingham's Market Place was invariably heaving, with frequent markets at the bottom of Angel Row (in the foreground) and on the main part of the Square. Trams were ubiquitous (five feature on this postcard, no. 364 in the 'Clumber' series). From 1905, Queen Victoria (on the right) presided over all that was going on. Goose Fair was held here until 1928. Hundreds, perhaps thousands of different postcard views were produced of this location throughout the 20th century - and, indeed, still are, as postcards continue to be popular. The Exchange Building (erected 1726) - with shops on the ground floor - was replaced by the current Council House in 1929. The photo below was taken at ground level, while the postcard above shows an elevated view.

Nottingham Market Place

Looking up Market Street, with three trams and Queen Victoria's statue in the picture on 'Clumber' postcard no. 127. The statue was built in marble by Albert Toft to commemorate the reign that ended with Victoria's death in 1901. It was unveiled by the Duchess of Portland on 28th July 1905 in front of a massive crowd. In 1953, though, it was moved to The Embankment because the road area needed enlarging to accommodate increasing traffic. At the start of Long Row on the right is the famous Griffin & Spalding department store, opened in 1846 and sold to Debenhams in 1944 - though it continued to trade under the original name until 1973. On the left of the picture is the Talbot, a pub opened in 1876 and sold to Yates's Wine Lodge in 1929. On its ground floor stood the King's Theatre, and later a cinema.

Long Row, Nottingham

The 17th century 'Black Boy Hotel', redesigned in 1887 by top Nottingham architect Watson Fothergill, was controversially demolished in 1970 to make way for a Littlewoods shop (now Primark) on what is now Smithy Row, but at the time of this postcard was part of an extended Long Row. An early motor car (one of only a very few around at the time) appears in the picture (registration no. AL 562). You might have expected this view, just round the corner from Hindley's shop, to have been among the first to figure in this series, but it came out as no. 139. This copy was posted at Radcliffe-on-Trent in 1910 and sent to Scarborough. Looking at the photo below, it's hard to say that the architecture has been improved.

The Poultry, Nottingham

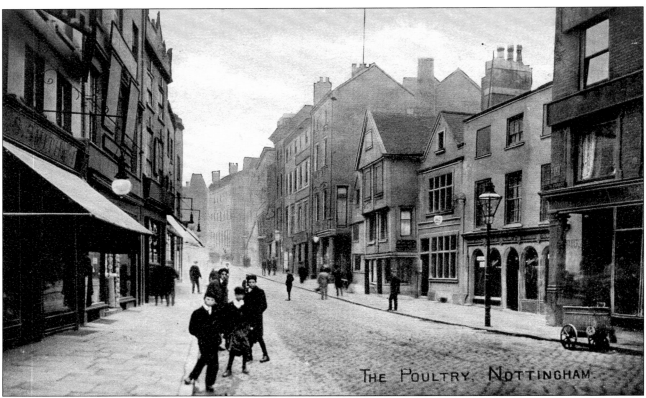

Cheapside is on the left of this postcard, no. 144, The Poultry, with the iconic 'Flying Horse Hotel' on the right. This ancient coaching inn was established in 1483, but was known as the 'Traveller's Rest' until the late 18th century, when it took the 'Flying Horse' name. Allowed to deteriorate during the 19th century, it was restored in 1935 and survived as a pub until 1989, when it became a shopping arcade - though, learning the lesson of the 'Black Boy' debacle in the 1960s, the facade was retained. It is now on the tram route through the city. The right-hand side has not changed significantly, but the left was totally redeveloped in 1929. Back in 1901, Nottingham's population was quoted in the census at 239,743. Biggest local industries at the time were lacemaking, silk, wool, machinery, iron foundries, breweries and tanneries. Boots, John Player and Raleigh Cycles were also becoming signficant employers.

The Hippodrome, Nottingham

THE HIPPODROME, NOTTINGHAM.

The 'Royal Hippodrome' at the corner of Wollaton and Goldsmith Streets was opened on 28th September 1908 as a variety theatre, one of the largest in Britain. This size may have contributed to its demise, for with the waning of interest in variety in the 1920s it became harder to fill and run at a profit. The Hippodrome was near the Theatre Royal and The Empire, and there was a hotel, the Clarendon, in between them, which presumably did very well out of performer and customer overnight stays. The Hippodrome was converted to cinema use in the 1950s but closed in 1971, being demolished the following year.

Before the Hippodrome occupied this site, it was the loction of Whitehall's factory, devastated by a fire in August 1905.

The site has been totally redeveloped and is now an Oriental food supermarket. The building's shape is recognisable but the impressive tower has gone. In front of the store is the Theatre Royal tram stop, which has a very regular service to Hucknall, Clifton, Phoenix Park and Beeston.

Theatre Royal and Empire, Nottingham

Card no. 93, showing two of the great theatres of Edwardian Nottingham. The still-thriving Theatre Royal opened in 1865 and has been refurbished and renewed several time since. The Nottingham Empire opened in 1898 and over the years attracted many of the great music hall performers. Max Miller, W.C. Fields, George Robey, Gracie Fields and Little Tich all appeared there. In the 1950s, pop stars such as Dickie Valentine and Lonnie Donegan played to packed houses. This is postcard no. 297, sent to Grimsby in August 1919. The Royal Concert Hall (opened in 1969), part of the Royal Centre, is to the right of the photo below. Had the picture been taken a few days later, the trees in leaf would have obscured the buildings.

Mansfield Road, Nottingham

Posted to Liverpool in September 1929 (did someone keep this for 20 years, or was the postcard series still on sale at this late date?!), card no. 131 shows a branch of Boots The Chemists on the left and a prominent advert for Player's 'Navy Cut' cigarettes, made, of course, in Nottingham. This is now a very busy road junction at the corner of Shakespeare Street and Mansfield Road, negotiated by frequent buses as well as cars - but not part of a current tram route.

Mechanics Hall, Nottingham

Card no. 374. The Mechanics' Hall was set up in 1837, with premises on St. James's Street until the institution set up in an impressive building at the corner of Burton and Milton Streets in the area that was part of Trinity Square. Originally called the Nottingham Mechanics Institute, it aimed to improve the knowledge of working men with classes, lectures, and performances of music, drama and readings. Famous people, including Charles Dickens, came along to speak or give readings. In the last century, it housed a cinema. This building was demolished in 1957 and replaced by Birkbeck House, which the Mechanics used, before relocating to a building on the corner of Shakespeare and North Sherwood Streets (smaller picture). Replicating this postcard picture is difficult because there is no longer the view up Burton Street (seen above) because of buildings nearer the camera. Burton Street itself has been much-narrowed. Replacing the Mechanics location now is TK Max. Our photo was also hampered

by traffic and street furniture, but on the plus side there are treesl

Milton Street, Nottingham

MILTON STREET, NOTTINGHAM.

This is card no. 134, showing Milton Street from its Parliament Street junction. A large pair of eyes on the right advertised Bain & Co.'s Eyesight Testing Rooms. Next to this, and nearest the camera, was the 'Milton's Head Hotel', which, along with other buildings on this road, was sold for demolition in 1969 and is now part of the Victoria Centre. Note also the tram standards in the centre of the road for holding the wires - one tram is heading away from the town centre. Today it's a busy bus route. The Intu Victoria Centre, dominated in this view by the John Lewis shop, is on the right of the photo, and just off picture is the always crowded road crossing, now controlled by traffic lights. In Edwardian times, a policeman would have sufficed at particularly busy times.

WESLEYAN CHAPEL.
MANSFIELD ROAD, NOTTINGHAM.

The foundation stone of the Wesleyan Chapel at the corner of Woodborough and Mansfield Roads was laid in May 1871. The chapel closed in 1940 and was sold to a Christian Science group, then later it was owned by the Emmanuel Gospel Church until 1973, when it was demolished. 'Clumber' postcard no. 152. The building that replaced it (right) currently accommodates The Dice Cup Board Game Café and the Nottingham Community Housing Association.

Mansfield Road, Nottingham.

One of the earliest 'Clumber' postcards, no. 3, posted at Collingham in August 1908. Today (right) this is the location of the Goose Fair roundabout. As can be seen on both postcards here, Mansfield Road was an important tram route to Sherwood and Mapperley.

Forest Recreation Ground, Nottingham

Locating the exact spots on The Forest where Albert Hindley took the photos for his postcards was a little tricky, but these scenes show (above, no. 106, sent to Leamington Spa in December 1906) the walkways just below Forest Road entrance; right - the entrance from Bentinck Road on postcard no. 368, posted from Nottingham in December 1907; below - one of the avenues on card no. 92, sent to Luton in August 1906. The Forest was once used for horse-racing before the current Nottingham (formerly Colwick) Racecourse was established. It is also a leisure (football and children's playground) facility, and the location of a park and ride site, with a tram stop adjacent. Since 1928, the Forest has hosted Goose Fair. In 1911 a massive gathering of children was organised to celebrate the Coronation

The Arboretum, Nottingham

Chinese-Bell
Nott^m Arboretum

Postcard no. 31, showing the Arboretum's famous Chinese bell (a replica; the original was taken to a regimental museum in Preston) and Crimean War cannon. The bell doesn't ring and the cannon don't fire, but it's a fun monument to climb onto!

Today (right) the scene is little-changed, though the trees obscure the view of the High School buildings behind the bell tower on the postcard. The Arboretum, opened in 1852, is well-maintained and a lovely park to walk around and relax in. It holds the statue of Chartist leader Feargus O'Connor and a bust of politician Samuel Morley. Originally the latter's statue stood outside the Theatre Royal, but when it was decided to move it to the Arboretum the statue was damaged in transit - it literally fell off the back of a lorry. Hence the bust was made as a substitiute.

The Aviary appeared on card no. 108. It has always been one of the park's great attractions. Today's cages are less ornate and, bizarrely, one of them holds plastic model birds in memory of the Aviary's longest-living inhabitant.

Nottingham High School

Nottingham High School's main building south facade on Waverley Street looks much the same as in the early 20th century, but this view is now enhanced by the war memorial and a very well-kept garden. Founded in 1513, the school relocated to Waverley Mount in 1868 and since then has expanded with a series of new buildings. Most recent addition is an impressive theatre. It became co-educational in 2015 - previously there were separate schools for boys and girls. Alumni include politicians Kenneth Clarke and Ed Balls, cricketer Reg Simpson, Sir Jesse Boot and John Player (founders of hugely successful local companies) and Albert Ball, first Royal Flying Corps winner of the Victoria Cross. His statue is in Nottingham Castle grounds. The school even has its own tram stop (also titled 'for The Arboretum'. Card no. 36.

Nottingham, Clumber Street and Albert Hindley's shop

It took Albert Hindley until postcard no. 336 to decide to publish one of the road that ran past his shop. So here is a busy Clumber Street with horse-drawn vehicles and smartly-dressed people. Clumber Street was and is the thoroughfare from the end of Long (Smithy) Row to Parliament Street, but it is now pedestrianised. This postcard was sent to Welllingborough in December 1909.

Below left: Hindley used the back of a postcard of Toton to advertise his products. He claimed over 600 designs, but probably produced only 450 of these himself.

Nottingham Castle

A view of Nottingham's iconic 19th century landmark from The Park Estate, taken from the intersection of Peveril Drive and Lenton Road. The Castle is in fact a 19th century grand house, built after the previous building was burned down by Reform Bill rioters in 1831. Further back, the original Norman Castle was dismantled by parliamentary forces in 1651 after the English Civil War - nearby is Standard Hill where Charles I raised his standard at the start of the war. It has been owned by Nottingham City Council since the late 19th century and has been a visitor attraction - museum, site for special events, attractive grounds. It is currently closed for a major refurbishment - the photo below shows it encased in protective material - and the promise of a spectacular experience. The Castle is due to re-open in 2020.

Nottingham Castle Entrance

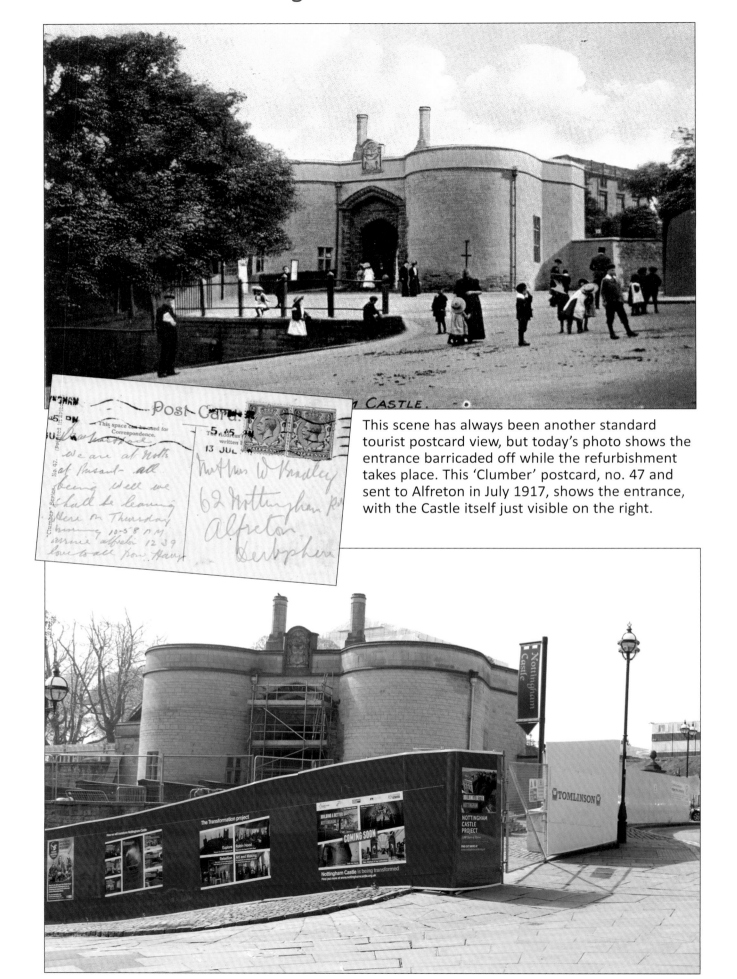

This scene has always been another standard tourist postcard view, but today's photo shows the entrance barricaded off while the refurbishment takes place. This 'Clumber' postcard, no. 47 and sent to Alfreton in July 1917, shows the entrance, with the Castle itself just visible on the right.

Sneinton Market

Sneinton held a very important regular outdoor market until Nottingham City Council moved the whole lot to the Victoria Centre and gave it a covered area. Postcard no. 166. The area subsequently became run down but in recent years big efforts have been made to regenerate it, with festivals, events and regular markets happening. Architect Patel Taylor was responsible for redesigning the square and today it looks extremely attractive, with the impressive Victoria Leisure Centre clock tower still overlooking the scene as it did at the start of the 20th century.

The Lace Market, Nottingham

The Lace Market was once the beating heart of business in Nottingham and the hub of the British Empire's lace industry. Though the industry has largely gone, the magnificent Victorian redbrick buildings put up by the lace merchants are still there and the area, a protected heritage site, has been sympathetically rebranded with interesting shops, businesses and restaurants. Today it is a lovely area to stroll through. Postcard no. 269 in Hindley's series shows female workers leaving the various businesses, walking down Stoney Street to where it meets Hollowstone and High Pavement. Stoney Street is no longer as packed with people as it once was!

THE LACE MARKET, NOTTINGHAM.

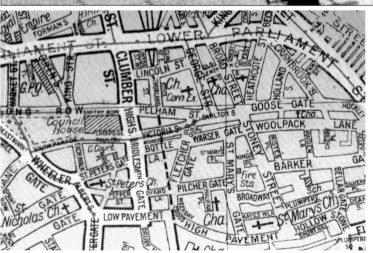

The Lace Market area (bordered by Goose Gate, Fletcher Gate and High Pavement) on a c.1925 Nottingham street plan published by Geographia and sold at Sisson & Parker's (once of Wheeler Gate).

Henry Kirke White (1785-1806) acquired something of a reputation in Nottingham, possibly exaggerated because of his early death at the age of 21, as a poet and hymn writer, and his birthplace and Wilford cottage were well-known locally at one time. A street in the Meadows was named after him. He wrote most of his poetry in his cottage, and apparently Byron and Shelley approved of his work, thought by some to be too provocative. Plagued by illness throughout his life, he'd aimed to be a lawyer despite his butcher father disapproving, and actually made it to St. John's College, Cambridge, where he died of consumption. The Exchange Arcade seen below was built in 1929 as part of the new Council House complex. Inside it is a plaque in relief commemorating the spot where he was born. Postcard no. 105.

Lister Gate, Nottingham

WALTER FOUNTAIN, LISTER GATE, NOTTINGHAM.

The Walter Fountain, erected by the son of John Walter M.P. after the latter's death in 1847. It was a 50-foot tower with four drinking fountains at the base, and stood just above what is now the entrance to Broad Marsh Shopping Centre. On the left of this picture ('Clumber' series no. 91, posted to Scarborough in October 1910) can be seen the 'Sawyer's Arms' pub and the 'Caledonian Hotel'. The scene below is almost unrecognisable, now pedestrianised and shaded by trees. The photographic postcard bottom left puts the scene into further context with a view looking from the end of Carrington Street and showing the Walter Fountain on the left.

The Postern Gate Inn

The Postern Gate was on the corner of the steep Drury Hill, controversially demolished to make way for the Broad Marsh Shopping Centre, and Middle Pavement. It was adjacent to what is now the upper entrance to the shopping centre. Postcard no. 135, posted in Nottingham in December 1916 and sent to Jacksdale. The photo above shows the closed top entrance to the shopping centre, currently being given a complete makeover. Below is a close-up of the signage there, with the Drury Hill street name indicator kept as a memento of the location's past history.

Midland Railway Station, Nottingham

Postcard no. 268 showing the interior of Midland Station, now the only one left in the city. The original station was built in 1848, and redesigned in 1904, since when it has remained pretty much the same at platform level - though the concourse had a make-over earlier this century. The bridge above carried the Great Central line to Loughborough and London. Now a structure above the station carries trams, and the pedestrian walkway beyond still exists. This card was posted at Mansfield in April 1927, sent back to Nottingham to an address on Trent Lane.

Queen's Walk, Nottingham

QUEEN'S WALK, NOTTINGHAM.

Card no. 257, with a view looking towards the railway station and with St. Mary's Church visible in the distance. The card was posted to Blackpool in August 1909 (isn't that the wrong way round?). Annie wrote: *"I hope you are enjoying yourself and having nice weather which it will go too quick for you my word if I catch you paddling..."* (sic.).

Today, the trams make an appropriate addition to the green surroundings so close to the city centre.

The top end of Queen's Walk on postcard no. 138, showing a more attractive view than the one today, when the top part has been enabled to accommodate road traffic. Postcard no. 138, posted at Shipley in West Yorkshire in April 1907. Postcards often travelled a long way and waited a long time before they went into the postal system!

QUEEN'S WALK, NOTTINGHAM.

Lenton Boulevard, Nottingham

Postcard no. 231. A tram crosses Gregory Boulevard along Radford Road on the Lenton-Radford route, introduced in September 1902. Services ceased in May 1934. By the end of 1902, 105 electric trams were ferrying passengers to Sherwood, Bulwell, Trent Bridge, St. Ann's, Mapperley and Wilford Road, and they proved extremely convenient and popular. The rise of motor buses and cars eventually rendered the trams redundant, but 68 years after the last tram ran in Nottingham, a new fleet began operation, and that initial system to Hucknall and Phoenix Park was then extended to Clifton, Beeston and Chilwell.

Edwards Lane, Sherwood

A very rural-looking Edwards Lane in 1904 is transformed by 2019 into a busy road on the eastern side of the City Hospital. Postcard no. 398, posted from Nottingham to Manchester in July 1913. This was one of those locations where it was very difficult to identify the exact spot where the original photograph was taken. The City Hospital is to the left of the photo.

Tram Sheds, Sherwood

One of the Edwardian tram depots was on Mansfield Road, Sherwood, as seen here on 'Clumber' series postcard no. 151. The card was posted at Mansfield, sent to Arnold with a query: *"Do you know anything of this?"*. The facility subsequently became a bus depot for Nottingham Corporation buses (the left-hand part stll is, though temporarily closed in the 1980s). The right-hand shed is now a branch of Wetherspoon's, named the 'Samuel Hall' after a local lace manufacturer. The tram depot was opened in 1901 on the site of Woodville Lodge, where an impressive drive led up to Woodville House.

MANSFIELD ROAD, SHERWOOD, NOTTINGHAM.

The fourth card in the series, posted from Nottingham to Huddersfield in October 1905. *"I expect you will know this view"*, wrote Harry. The church on the left has been demolished and replaced by a new Methodist Church building. Further on, Mansfield Road in Sherwood is quickly becoming a go-to location for people wanting to eat out.

Sherwood Railway Station

Postcard no. 6 in the series, posted at Nottingham to a local address in February 1906. Sherwood station was on the short-lived Nottingham Suburban Railway. The tunnel in the distance, seen on the next postcard, went beneath part of Woodthorpe Park. The line, which short-cutted the more tortuous one via Gedling, opened in 1889, financed by a group of Nottingham businessmen. There were two other stations on the line - Thorneywood and St. Ann's Well, and the journey from Nottingham Victoria to Daybrook took just 14 minutes in 1910 (journey by bus today is double that). The stations were all closed in 1916 as a wartime economy measure, never to be re-opened, though passenger trains used the route until 1931. A model of a tunnel and train, and a mosaic, in Woodthorpe Park (see next page) is a reminder of the line. The photo below was taken from a lower viewpoint than the postcard because the view from the bridge (right) reveals not much! Two tower blocks, Winchester and Woodthorpe Courts, now stand where the station once was, and more low-rise flats are currently being constructed. The photo below right shows a train leaving the station, possibly in 1951, when a one-off enthusiasts' special used the route.

Sherwood Railway Tunnel

SHERWOOD NOTTINGHAM

'Clumber' series card no. 5, showing the entrance to the tunnel beneath part of Woodthorpe Park. To the right of the picture (and as seen on previous postcard), a branch line went up a steep incline to Mapperley brickworks.

Left: the tunnel entrance today, blocked off. Below: the mosaic above the tunnel and the model at the northern end of Woodthorpe Park, commemorating the Nottingham Suburban Railway. Quite a lot of the old railway architecture still exists in the area, despite the obliteration of Sherwood station.

Tram Terminus, Mapperley

TRAM TERMINUS, MAPPERLEY, NOTTINGHAM.

Mapperley tram terminus at the top of Porchester Road seen on card no. 149. This was posted at Nottingham in August 1906, sent to a Skegness address. Services to Mapperley began in May 1902 and ran until February 1936. The route was the most hilly and difficult in the whole Nottingham network. Services ran from here to Trent Bridge via the Market Place.

Daybrook Church

DAYBROOK CHURCH, NOTTS

Un-numbered postcard, postally used from Bulwell in March 1906 and sent to Liverpool. St. Paul's Church dominates the scene on Mansfield Road, Daybrook. Now a Grade II listed building, it was designed by architect John Pearson in the late 19th century and consecrated in February 1896. The spire runs to 150ft. The tranquil scene above emphasises the difference a century makes. Today constant traffic makes road crossing - never mind ambling along - dangerous.

Carnegie Library, Arnold

One of several Carnegie-funded libraries that existed in Nottinghamshire, Arnold's, on Nottingham Road near the junction of what is now Arnot Hill Road, was demolished in 1981. The architect was William Higginbottom, who designed other buildings in the town. The replacement building is a branch of Wilko's, and the architecture is not quite so impressive. The library was opposite the Arnold branch of the Co-operative Society, now a Wetherspoon's, 'The Ernehale', whose interior decor reflects nicely the history of the area. Our photo, looking towards Front Street, has a more distant perspective than the postcard to take in the wider picture. Postcard no. 306, posted from Arnold to Newark in September 1908.

Thackeray's Lane, Arnold

This postcard, no. 395, was sent from Nottingham to Grantham on Christmas Eve 1910. The railway bridge, which was demolished in 1973, was on the Nottingham Suburban Railway. Today, Buckingham Road is on the right and there is a roundabout at the spot where five roads meet and the railway bridge crossed the road.

Bizarrely, the card was posted to a Mrs Thackeray, who lived at St. Peter's Hill, Grantham!

THACKERAY'S LANE
ARNOLD, NOTTS.

POST CARD.
NOTTINGHAM

This space can be used for Correspondence.

The Address only to be written here.

DEC 24 10

Many thanks for the lovely Calendar - also thank Dorothy for her letter
E. E. P.

Mrs Thackeray
20 St Peter's Hill
Grantham

Gedling Village

Another card where local children were co-opted to add some life to the picture. No. 329 in the series, it was posted with New Year wishes at Nottingham in November 1905 to New Zealand. This required the application of a penny stamp, double the inland rate. The card was actually redirected to New South Wales where it was delivered to Mr. Wilkinson at the second address that was suggested. Not bad value for a penny!

Gedling Railway Station

The Station, Gedling, Notts.

Gedling station (actually called Gedling & Carlton) opened in 1875 and was on the old Great Northern line which looped from Netherfield & Colwick station up to Daybrook and Bulwell. It had a frequent service to Nottingham in 1910, and even a very regular schedule on Sundays. The station was closed in April 1960, though, with competition from buses and cars making the line unviable. This postcard was sent to Stockport in August 1906. The original station building (the photo below left shows it from the road side) is currently owned by a youth group, though is apparently on the market. The view above has gone completely, the trackbed taken over by vegetation, and our best replica photo effort is shown below. The station building can just be seen through the forest! Rob took the photo after clambering through dense undergrowth.

Gedling and Carlton station was on the Great Northern line that ran from Nottingham Victoria to Basford and Bulwell. Some 14 passenger trains a day called, with the last train from Nottingham leaving at 10.50 and arriving at Gedling a quarter of an hour later. It closed completely in 1960, a few years before even Dr. Beeching could get his hands on it.

Burton Joyce

Burton Joyce has seen plenty of changes in the past century, notably the construction of a by-pass. This is Main Street in 1906, when it was common to see cows and sheep on the road. A number of farms were very close to the village centre. Card no. 75 in the 'Clumber' series, posted at Nottingham in August 1907 and sent to Wilford Grove. Despite the by-pass, Main Street today is still difficult to negotiate because of the number of motor cars parked along its length.

Burton Joyce Railway Station

Burton Joyce railway station is on the Nottingham to Lincoln line, which opened on 4th August 1846. On the postcard above (no. 174) the goods yard and sidings are on the left in the distance, with the signal box to the right. In 1906 fifteen passenger trains in each direction called on weekdays, with just a couple on Sundays. The postcard was posted to Bridlington from Nottingham in August 1906. Today the station buildings and signalbox have gone, leaving a very basic facility, but a regular passenger service is still available. Here a train bound for Nottingham is approaching the platform.

Lambley Lane, Burton Joyce

Crow Park Farm on Lambley Lane, Burton Joyce. The barn has been put to many uses in its lifetime, including a garage and now a doctor's surgery. This postcard, no. 173 in the series, was posted at Nottingham in September 1908, mailed to Wisbech. This part of the lane, near the old main street in Burton Joyce, has been extensively developed with housing. The lane doesn't provide access to Lambley any more.

Lowdham Station. APPROACH. NOTTINGHAM.

The signal box on the right still exists, but is no longer functional. The present owners of Station House, the prominent building on the left, are currently negotiating to buy the signal box and install it in their garden area. The small structure just to the left of the crossing was the Lamp Room where porters would house equipment. Off to the left now is a new housing estate, 'The Sidings'. The station was opened in 1846. This is postcard no. 179 in the series, and quite unusually devoid of any people.

Epperstone

Card no. 263, posted from the village to Cricklewood in September 1907. Epperstone, with a population of 362 in 1901, once had a paper mill. This view, looking towards the village centre, was taken on the original main road out of the village heading north.

Bulcote Church

Bulcote Church NOTTS

Bulcote, near Burton Joyce, was home to another famous postcard publisher, J.H. Scott. This example of card no. 177 was posted from Nottingham to Lenton in March 1907. Just 93 people lived here when this postcard was published. Holy Trinity Church, on a hill a little away from the village, was built and consecrated in 1862, replacing the original 13th century church that was destroyed in a violent thunderstorm. It is separated from the main part of the village by the main A612 road to Southwell. Bulcote, like so many small Nottinghamshire villages, has no shops - nor does it have a pub, which is slightly more unusual. The bus stop and shelter in the photo below are the only indication that anything has changed.

Woodborough Church

Woodborough Church stood proudly in the street in Edwardian days, but is now much more shaded by trees, so taking the comparative photo was challenging. This is card no. 365, sent to Southwell in September 1910. It shows the only forms of transport as a bicycle and a horse. The sender wrote *"We live in the row of houses the same side as the church. We are getting on fairly well"*. Over 700 potential worshippers lived in the village in the early 20th century. St. Swithun's Church has a 14th century chancel while the west tower was built in the 13th. Woodborough was once an important centre for the framework knitting industry.

Oxton Church

St. Peter and St. Paul's Church has a Norman doorway and window, and stands impressively on the main road through the village. Card no. 250. With a population of 455 in Edwardian days, that has increased a little to 568 now.

Locating this pub was tricky, but in fact it stood on the site of the current 'Ye Olde Bridge Inn' and bore the same name. The current building is at a different alignment to the original. 'Three Lane Ends' refers to the junction of the roads to Southwell, Nottingham and Ollerton. In the early 20th century Oxton had four pubs, including the 'Young Oak' and the 'Old Oak', which were opposite each other on Water Lane. This runs along a stream through the village, at one end of which is a quite exciting ford. Apparently this is closed to traffic for a while each March so that toads can breed. Card no. 249. The 'Bridge' has just been refurbished and is one of the two remaining pubs, the other being the 'Old Green Dragon'.

Lambley Church

LAMBLEY CHURCH. NOTTS.

No. 121 in the series. Holy Trinity Church at Lambley is one of the few almost entirely perpendicular village churches in the county, and the oldest part, the west tower, dates from the 12th century. In Edwardian times, the village had a population of 770, while now it is over 1,200. It still has shops and a couple of pubs. Today from the same angle the church is almost blotted out by houses and trees. Most of the buildings to the left of the church on the postcard are still there, albeit obscured from our vantage point. Lambley, incidentally, had the most through traffic of any village we visited, being on a short cut (avoiding Nottingham) from Lowdham to Arnold.

Calverton, Main Street

MAIN STREET, CALVERTON, NOTTS.

On the right is 64 Main Street, now a fish and chip shop, Calverton Fish Bar. On the left is the Baptist Chapel, just after 99 Main Street. This is 'Clumber' card no. 620, and when this was published Calverton's population was 1,159 - now it is just over 7,000. Most of that growth occurred after the opening of Calverton Colliery in 1952. That closed in 1993, but re-opened after being bought by RJB Mining, which gave the pit a five-year reprieve. Calverton is now mainly a commuter village, though there are some small industrial estates. A claim to fame is the fact that William Lee, probable inventor of the stocking-frame, lived in the village.

BURTON ROAD, CARLTON, NOTTS.

Hindley published a number of postcards with white borders, but they don't provide such a full-on image. This one (no. 397) of Burton Road at Carlton shows a number of locals gathered for the photo. Today, the trees in the picture have gone, and street furniture is more prominent. The road is still relatively quiet thanks to the by-pass. The postcard was sent to King Street locally (and was probably delivered the same day as it was posted) in February 1908. The sender ('M') wrote *"Dear Madge. I thought you would like this view. How would it be to live in this little spot? Try & take me for a walk in the morning. I always feel so much better when out with you alone... ring me up at 10.15... did you enjoy your Ovaltine?"* Not many people had a telephone then!

Carlton, Railway Crossing

Carlton railway station on the line from Nottingham to Lincoln is well-used today. The level crossing is still there, with a regular build-up of waiting cars in contrast to the postcard above (no. 11), with its charming content of bicycles and a horse and carriage. The signal box has been removed. On today's photo, the buildings on the left in the background are the 'Fox and Hounds' pub and the Tommy Thompson School of Boxing.

Colwick Hall

Colwick Hall dates from the 14th century, and between c.1500 and 1660 was owned by the Byron family before their move to Newstead Abbey. Then the Musters family bought it, renovating and redesigning it c.1775. The Hall was damaged by Reform Bill rioters in 1831 (when they also burned down Nottingham Castle) and sold to Nottingham Racecourse in 1892, when part of it became a public house and the rest accommodation for jockeys and grooms. Nottingham Corporation bought it in 1965, but the building fell into disrepair for a while. It is now a hotel and wedding venue. The roof is more austere now than in its 1906 appearance. Postcard no. 188, sent to Radford in February 1906.

Colwick Road, Nottingham

Postcard no. 363, posted in Nottingham in August 1907 and sent to an address on Great Alfred Street in the city. Emma wrote to Mr. Stevens: *"Don't let John get the best of you this week. I am not there to help you"*. The postcard shows a very quiet Colwick Road with a tram on the Basford-Colwick route, established in March 1907 - so the postcard must have been published very soon after that. The railway bridge in the background carried passengers on the Nottingham Suburban line on their way to Daybrook via Sherwood. No trace of the bridge exists today.

Colwick Race Course

Now known more realistically as Nottingham Racecourse, the facility has had its main stand totally redeveloped since the beginning of the 20th century. The racehorse 'Wild Fox' is quoted as the winner of the race just having taken place in the picture above on 'Clumber' series postcard no. 87. Nottingham Racecourse was originally located on the Forest Recreation Ground, but moved to its present site in Colwick Park in 1892. The course caters for flat racing only, though it staged National Hunt meetings until 1996. It once had its own railway station.

Colwick Crossing

Colwick Crossing, Notts.

Colwick Crossing is still used on the line from Nottingham to Grantham via Netherfield, Radcliffe and Bingham. This is one of the most common Edwardian picture postcard views outside the city centre. It is no. 212 in Hindley's series. This example was posted at Radcliffe-on-Trent and sent to Grantham in April 1907. The signal box is no longer there. The photographer lived dangerously but was massively helped by the closure of the crossing while a train went past!

Colwick Road and Wood

Colwick Rd & Wood, Nottingham.

One of Hindley's earliest postcards, no. 9, of the tram terminus at Colwick, with Colwick Woods on the left of the picture. This is just the other side of the railway level crossing from the previous image, and the same house can be seen in the picture. Postcard sent to Cambridge in September 1907. The card on page 53 shows a scene a little nearer Nottingham. The photo below is hardly inspiring, but that is part of the charm of recreating these scenes!

Netherfield & Colwick Railway Station

COLWICK STATION. NOTTS.

This station was originally called Colwick when opened in 1878, but in Edwardian times was called Netherfield. In 1925 this was changed to Netherfield & Colwick, and back to Netherfield in 1974. The impressive station buildings and canopies have now been replaced by a single shelter. Today's passenger services are limited, and the station is used by an average of just 23 people a day, far fewer than were waiting for this Nottingham-bound train in 1905 on this 'Clumber' postcard no. 12.

Taking a photograph from the same angle as Albert Hindley did is difficult today, as the view is blocked by hedges, so we've provided a platform view as well.

Basford Crossing

Basford Crossing, Nottingham

Over a century on, and the trams are back! This, one of Hindley's best postcard views, is no. 168 in the 'Clumber' series, and shows a tram from Bulwell Nottingham-bound and a goods train heading in the same direction on the Midland line. Today, the tram route parallels the railway track for much of the way up to Hucknall, and a stop has been created here at David Lane. We'll gloss over the wisdom of the duplicate transport facility (wasn't that why Richard Beeching closed many lines?) and ponder on how Nottingham is one of the far-sighted and fortunate few cities to have re-introduced trams. The photo was taken from the attractive red bridge spanning the railway.

Ladies' Pavilion, Bulwell Golf Links

LADIES' PAVILION, BULWELL GOLF LINKS, NOTTINGHAM.

As far back as 1887 the Notts Golf Club established links on Bulwell Forest, extending the initial seven-hole course to eighteen holes in 1894. Notts GC moved to Hollinwell, near Mansfield, in 1900, and two years later Bulwell Forest Golf Club was founded. Notts Ladies' Golf Club was founded in 1891 and had their own clubhouse here, though they too moved to Hollinwell in 1901. Their separate pavilion at Bulwell Forest continued to be used, and Albert Hindley photographed it in 1906, though all the players on the card appear to be male. This postcard, no. 157 in the series, was posted from Bulwell to Sleaford in October 1906. Ladies' golf was booming at the start of the 20th

century, and it's good to know Bulwell was in the vanguard. The Ladies' Pavilion in 1906 was on the other side of the (incredibly quiet) Hucknall Road (below), along with the Artisans' (working men's) clubhouse. On the course side of the road was the Professionals' (doctors, lawyers, accountants) clubhouse. The current one (below left) was modelled on the design of the Ladies' Pavilion, dismantled long ago. The site now houses the premises of Saxon Electrical Suppliers (left, just visible in the trees).

The postcard below is no. 153 in the 'Clumber' series. It was posted from Nottingham to Stoke Ferry in May 1908.

BULWELL GOLF LINKS, NOTTINGHAM.

Bulwell Hall

BULWELL HALL, NOTTS.

Bulwell Hall was built in 1770 by John Newton and known locally as 'Pye Wipe Hall'. His family occupied it until 1864, when it was bought by Samuel Cooper. Last century, it was used successively as a sanatorium, approved school and Italian prisoner of war camp. It was demolished in 1958 after mining subsidence added to damage done during the war. The clubhouse of Nottingham City Golf Club (originally established in 1910) now occupies the site, and the photos here show it from two angles to cover the possible alignment of the Hall. Postcard no. 324, posted from Bulwell to Giltbrook in November 1910.

Market Place, Bulwell

MARKET PLACE, BULWELL, NOTTINGHAM.

Card no. 154 shows an almost deserted Market Place at Bulwell, with just a solitary tram at the terminus and a few pedestrians. The scene looks much more lively today! Bulwell is still served by trams, and the current stop for the town centre is a hundred yards to the right of where the photograph was taken. Important industries at the start of the 20th century were quarrying, mining and framework knitting. The Edwardian service to Bulwell was the second route in Nottingham to open, in July 1901, and it ran until May 1934.

On the left of the postcard is the 'Horse & Groom' public house. When this closed, the name was taken by the pub currently near Moorgreen Garden Centre. Card no. 62 in the series, posted at Kimberley to a Doncaster address in July 1909. Nuthall (the spelling on the postcard is different but either is acceptable) had fewer than 600 people living in it in 1906. Today the M1 motorway runs right past the village, which is noted for its three large and impressive ponds.

Known as Hucknall Torkard until 1915, the town is the final resting place of Lord Byron (interred in the Parish Church), and various buildings in the area carry a reminder of the name, including the Byron cinema and bingo hall. One of the three railway stations formerly in the town was named 'Hucknall Byron'. Un-numbered postcard, sent from Hucknall to Surfleet in September 1907.

Market Place, Hucknall

Not only has Albert Hindley assembled a collection of local children to Hucknall Market Place on the grand occasion of his photographing it, he seems to have also arranged a couple of horse and cart owners to pose, too. The Zachariah Green drinking fountain (see next page) is prominent on the left. In contrast to the brilliantly stage-managed crowd scene on Hindley's postcard, we managed to persuade just one local to stand still on a chilly morning in April 2019. Over 15,000 people lived in Hucknall in the Edwardian era, many working in the extensive nearby collieries.

Zachariah Green's House, Hucknall

Zachariah Green, a famous local benefactor, lived on Beardall Street in the nearest house. Born in 1817, he was a philanthropist who dispensed medical advice and supplies to poor people in nearby towns and villages. His work earned him a huge reputation and made him an iconic figure in Hucknall. He died in 1897 but his work was carried on by his son, grandson and grand-daughter. After his death, a memorial in the form of a granite drinking fountain was put up in Hucknall Market Place and relocated to Titchfield Park in 1922. Zachariah is buried in St. Mary Magdalene churchyard in Hucknall. Alas, his house is no more, having been demolished, along with its neighbour. A nursing home (just visible in the main picture and inset), opened in May 2019, stands on part of the land. Card no. 264 in the series.

Derby Road, Eastwood

DERBY ROAD. EASTWOOD NOTTS.

Derby Road in Eastwood, looking from the north, is now much more developed with housing. The old coal mining town is famous as the place where the Midland Railway was set up (at the 'Sun Inn') and as the birthplace of writer D.H. Lawrence - there is a museum dedicated to him in the town. Population at the time the postcard was published was just under 5,000. Postcard no. 293, sent to Nottingham in October 1908.

Victoria Embankment, Nottingham

Victoria Embankment Approch
Nottingham

This is Rob the photographer's favourite comparative photo, showing as it does how the trees have matured over 113 years. Postcard no. 267 posted from Nottingham to another city address in January 1907. The picture shows the entrance to the splendid embankment from the northern end of Trent Bridge. Every August this area becomes part of the annual Riverside Festival.

Masonic Hall, West Bridgford

Masonic Hall, West Bridgford.

Albert Hindley used a different lens to our photographer Rob as both pictures were taken from the same spot yet the Masonic Hall on the south bank of the River Trent appears larger. In the photo, one of the Trent pleasure cruisers is passing. The river is also used regularly by the local rowing and canoe clubs, and the north bank hosts the huge Riverside Festival on the first weekend of August. Postcard no. 463, posted to Sutton-on-Sea in August 1911.

Suspension Bridge over the River Trent

New Suspension Bridge. Nottingham

Card no. 604. The magnificent (for a footbridge) suspension bridge was built in 1906 to carry water supply pipes from Wilford Hill reservoir, and to provide a pedestrian route into town, though it remained closed on Sundays for many years after this. The postcard photo must have been taken shortly after it was opened. It has been renovated in the past few years, and since its re-opening has become a popular place for securing love locks on the railings. The bridge provides a lovely place to stand and contemplate the superb view towards Trent Bridge. Taking a photo from exactly the same viewpoint was not possible because of the developments on the south bank. Note the distinctive green roof of County Hall on the right of the photo below.

Trent Bridge, Nottingham

Trent Bridge is the iconic river crossing south of the city, once the main artery going south until Clifton Bridge (a mile and a half to the west) opened in 1958. To improve traffic flow even more, the old railway bridge 300 yards east was converted for road traffic use in 1982. This bridge can be seen in the distance on both the postcard and the photo. Card no. 298, posted in London in 1918.

The first crossing over the Trent here dates back to the 10th century, and a second 12th century edifice lasted - with many repairs - until the 19th. A small section of this bridge is still extant today on the south bank. The current version was begun in 1868 and opened in 1871. It was widened in the mid-1920s. The bridge has given its name to the nearby cricket ground and the Trent Bridge Inn. Rob's photograph replaces the rowing boat on the postcard with an elegant swan.

To the right of the postcard, a grand international exhibition had been held a few years previously, but it was destroyed by a massive fire on 4th July 1904.

Lover's Walk, West Bridgford

LOVER'S WALK, TRENT BRIDGE.
NOTTINGHAM.

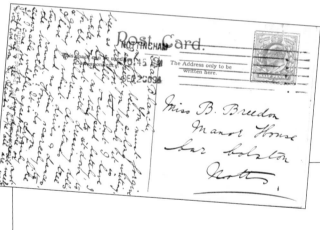

Card no. 192, posted to Car Colston in December 1909. Lover's Walk was a secluded area then, with plenty of tree cover for the romantically-inclined (even comic postcards featured it!), but today the cover is all for the houses to the right. This picture gives a splendid view of Trent Bridge and the Town Arms (on the left, once the toll house for Trent Bridge), now transformed after many recent incarnations into the 'Brewhouse and Kitchen'.

Patrick Road, West Bridgford

The Wesleyan Church on Patrick Road - just off Musters Road - has been extensively rebuilt since this 'Clumber' postcard (no. 260) was produced 114 years ago, but the distinctive tower with its pagoda-like top still exists. This card was sent from Nottingham to Skegness in February 1911. *"I wish I was at Skeggy now"*, wrote the sender.

Trent Boulevard, West Bridgford

This postcard (no. 259) was sent to an address in Coventry on Christmas Eve 1907, bearing Christmas wishes to Georgie. It would have been delivered on 25th December. The scene is largely unchanged today, except, of course, for the number of motor cars. Reassuringly, the same postbox is still there! This street is part of the Lady Bay area, which is rapidly becoming very fashionable.

Embankment & Railway Bridge, West Bridgford

EMBANKMENT & RAILWAY BRIDGE, WILFORD.

The Great Central railway bridge over the Trent near Wilford on postcard no. 290, sent to Lincoln in September 1909. The line, from Nottingham Victoria to Marylebone, was the alternative route from the Midlands to London. There were actually three components to the structure, over the river, embankment and road. Only the foundation stones can now be seen. Part of the embankment can still be spotted in Iremonger Park, and the trackbed then runs through to Wilford Lane parallel with the tram tracks. Part of it is then under the tram route up to the Ruddington Lane stop. To take the photo, we walked to the northern end of the park, where there is also a great view of the old Toll Bridge.

Melton Road, Edwalton

MELTON ROAD, EDWALTON, NOTTS.

'Clumber' series postcard no. 241, posted at Ruddington in October 1910, sent to Mapperley. Just up the lane on the right is Edwalton railway station, closed to passengers in 1941. It is surprising that a station was built here for a village with 230 souls rather than West Bridgford, which had a population 28 times bigger. Perhaps the Midland railway felt Bridgford was too close to Nottingham (just a mile from the city station), or perhaps it had an eye on the goods traffic potential from local farms. Why Hindley chose to portray this near-empty scene rather than walk another 100 yards and photograph the station is not clear, either. The house on the left has been replaced, but the one peeping out from the trees on the postcard is no longer visible from the same vantage point.

Main Road, Plumtree

MAIN ROAD. PLUMTREE, NOTT^M

'Clumber' postcard no. 335, posted at Nottingham. Plumtree's population in 1906 was 230, but it boasted a railway station, and later the local telephone exchange was sited there. In Edwardian days two pubs stood virtually opposite each other - the 'Farmer's Arms' (seen on this postcard) and the 'Griffin', currently closed for refurbishment. Today the former is a private house and hardly visible from the road, while the 'Griffin' is the building behind the tree in the distance on the right.

Bunny Lane, Keyworth

BUNNY LANE, KEYWORTH, NOTTS

In 1904 Keyworth had a population of 789, and was largely centred around the church and the roads leading away from that. Today that part of the village is a conservation area. The population rose to over 8,000 after intense housing development in the 1950-80 period, but fell to 6,733 by the 2011 census. Projected extra housing will see another large increase soon, though. This is postcard no. 334 (one of just three that Hindley published of Keyworth) posted at Nottingham in 1907. It shows Manor Farm, in 1906 owned by the Eggleston family. It survived until 1968, in its later days operated as a plant nursery. Today's photo shows the space now used for a fitness club, Primary Care Centre and car park. The parish church of St. Mary Magdalene, its distinctive 'coffee pot' tower and spire - unique in Britain - clearly visible on the postcard, has been overshadowed by the late 20th century builds.

Bradmore Church

Postcard no. 308, posted, bizarrely, from Bexhill-on-Sea to St. Leonards-on-Sea in December 1908. 'E.B.' wrote to 'Dearest Sarah': *"I really don't think I can face it tonight so don't expect me. Hope you are well"*. The expectation was that the postcard would be delivered the same day, which was normal over short distances.

Services are still held at Bradmore's Church of England building. Only the spire survives from the 13th and 14th century original after a disastrous fire in 1705.

Once a farming community, Bradmore's farm buildings have been largely converted to private residential use. It had at one time two windmills, and the many tradespeople in the village made it largely a self-sufficient community.

Main Road, Bradmore

In Hindley's day Bradmore (population 230 then, now about 330) was a pretty quiet place, though it did have a shop, post office and two public houses, all now gone. It lies on the now very busy A60 road, and taking the photograph below was hazardous! 'Clumber' postcard no. 301.

Church Street, Ruddington

Church St, Ruddington, Notts.

Those children on the postcard wouldn't hang around in the middle of Church Street today! The scene now is dominated by cars parking to use the Co-operative Society shop - and others! The Happy Garden Chinese takeaway on the right provides a splash of colour - as, indeed, do some of the cars! This is postcard no. 344, sent from Ruddington to Loughborough in December 1908. At the end of the street is St. Peter's Church. In Edwardian days Ruddington had almost 2,500 inhabitants, making it then the largest village in the south of the county. It had a railway station from 1900 on the Great Central line to London that closed in 1967. The local Rushcliffe Country Park now houses a heritage railway that uses the track that was a branch from the GC main line to the Ministry of Defence depot that once occupied the location.

Wilford Road, Ruddington

This card, sent to a resident of The Park in Nottingham in July 1906, shows a very quiet Wilford Road in the Edwardian era. Today this thoroughfare, hardly widened at all, is one of Ruddington's several bottlenecks, with parked cars reducing the road to a voluntary one-way-at-a-time route. The old chapel on the right is now a private house. The message included *"Pleased to come to tea with you tomorrow Thursday afternoon & then to the Show in the evening"* (at The Empire? Theatre Royal?). The road here diverges where the white van is in the photo below, going left to Clifton and straight on to Wilford. Two miles in the Wilford direction is the tram stop Ruddington Lane, which is not too convenient for the village's over 7,000 inhabitants.

Costock Village

At the turn of the 20th century, when this postcard was published, Bradley Truman was mine host of this once-popular pub in Costock on the main road from Nottingham to Loughborough, now a quiet country road after the A60 was diverted to the west. He made it a haven for music hall performers and many famous names such as Harry Lauder, Marie Lloyd and Dan Leno paid visits. It closed in 2015 and has been turned into residential use. 'Clumber' series card no. 377, posted at Nottingham and sent to an address in the city in June 1908.

Built in 1766, Costock Mill on the road towards East Leake survived until 1921, when a local farmer persuaded the owner, lord of the manor Colonel Whyte, to let him destroy it so new farm buildings could be erected. It was still in working order up to at least 1910. Postcard no. 379, posted at Keyworth in July 1912. *"I was very pleased with your PC you sent me"*, wrote Fanny to Doris at Ambleside. Nothing remains of the mill today, but a cottage stands on the site now (obviously called Windmill Cottage!), part of Elms Farm.

Gamston Village

Gamston village was once on the main road, but is now tucked away magically within a large housing development that has grown up bordering the A52 and the A606. Card no. 54 was sent from Cropwell Butler to Twickenham in January 1908.

Holme Pierrepont Lock

THE LOCK. HOLME PIERREPONT

Holme Pierrepont Lock featured on Hindley's postcard no. 25. The scene below looks in some ways similar but in fact big changes have taken place here. A new lock, now known as Holme Lock no. 5, was built in 1921; the lock-keeper's house dates from 1947. This is now adjacent to the huge leisure

facility known as the National Watersports Centre - a path to the right of the photo takes you through to it. To the left of the house on the photo below, major works are being undertaken to improve the lock area still further. On the postcard above, a barge belonging to the Trent Navigation Co. is moored by the lock.

COLWICK LOCK. NOTTS.

Before the transition in the area to the watersports facility and the new lock, there was another lock at the other end of what was known as Holme Cut. This was Colwick, seen on 'Clumber' postcard no.16, posted at Maidenhead in March 1906 and sent back to a Netherfield address! Gerty, who wrote the card to her mother and brother to say she'd arrived safely in Maidenhead - *"lovely weather"*, was obviously given the card pre-stamped so she could let her family know of her safe arrival.

Ferry & Boathouse, Radcliffe-on-Trent

Postcard no. 240, posted from Nottingham to Portobello in September 1907. It shows the Wharf House on the right and the boathouse on the left. The railway bridge over Wharf Lane can be seen to the right, and the ferryman (John Bell) is in his boat - albeit without customers. A crossing cost one penny. The Wharf House was occupied by the wharfinger and ferryman. Built in 1820, it replaced a previous building, and was once at the heart of a thriving trade in goods, particularly coal and lime, which were regularly landed at the Wharf. Once the railway came, this trade declined. All the buildings on the postcard have been demolished and the area is occupied by a caravan site. To reach this spot required a three-mile bike ride/walk. In 1904 Hindley would, I suppose, have asked the ferryman to take him across!

Radcliffe-on-Trent Church

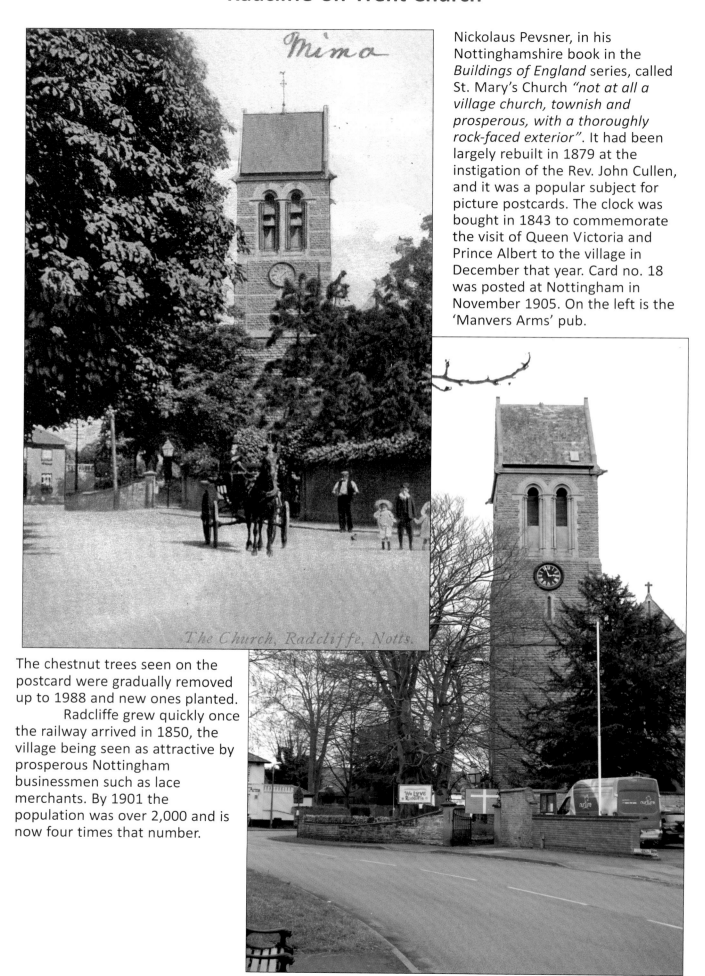

Nickolaus Pevsner, in his Nottinghamshire book in the *Buildings of England* series, called St. Mary's Church *"not at all a village church, townish and prosperous, with a thoroughly rock-faced exterior"*. It had been largely rebuilt in 1879 at the instigation of the Rev. John Cullen, and it was a popular subject for picture postcards. The clock was bought in 1843 to commemorate the visit of Queen Victoria and Prince Albert to the village in December that year. Card no. 18 was posted at Nottingham in November 1905. On the left is the 'Manvers Arms' pub.

The chestnut trees seen on the postcard were gradually removed up to 1988 and new ones planted.

Radcliffe grew quickly once the railway arrived in 1850, the village being seen as attractive by prosperous Nottingham businessmen such as lace merchants. By 1901 the population was over 2,000 and is now four times that number.

Bingham, Market Square

MARKET SQUARE BINGHAM, NOTTS.

Card no. 117, posted at Nottingham in September 1905. *"Don't go and say you have got this one. I don't think you have"* - obviously sent to a collector! The town of Bingham's population at the time the postcard was published was just over 1,600; now it is over 9,000 and rising. It has plenty of small businesses that operate here, and the Market Square is at the centre of a bustling shopping economy. The food market each Thursday is a big attraction. The Butter Cross is a really fine example of the genre, which still exists in many places across the country.

Whatton in the Vale

Three miles east of Bingham, Whatton had a population of 253 in 1904. This quiet view - no. 207 in Hindley's series - is little-changed today. The village church (St. John's, which Pevsner said had been *"architecturally almost wholly ruined by several restorations and alterations"*) is to the left of the picture.

Nottingham Road, Cropwell Bishop

The Wheatsheaf pub is on the left and still serving today. Beyond it, on the left, today, are a sandwich shop, hairdresser's and butcher's, once owned by Mr. Barlow but now the shop of Gary Jowett, who I knew when we both played rugby for Keyworth. On the right of the postcard is the chimney of a steam-powered corn mill. The mill and chimney, built in 1860 by William Saxton, were destroyed in an explosion in 1910, severely injuring the owner John Billings and worker George Johnson. The remains were cleared a couple of years later. The postcard (no. 236) shows the pub offering 'Good stabling', the need for which is underlined by the presence of the carriage in the picture. The card was posted to Huddersfield in August 1911 - *"I am enjoying my holiday & no time for writing"*. Sending a postcard was a useful time-saving substitute for writing a letter!

The 1758-built property seen on the left of the postcard was demolished sometime during the last century. The current owner, Patrick Briggs, appears on the photo below, leaning against his wall. The 'Clumber' series postcard, no. 238, was posted to Retford in October 1906. Cropwell Butler had a population of almost 500 in Edwardian days.

Kinoulton

Postcard no. 89, posted at Nottingham in August 1919, sent to Cricklewood. Kinoulton, with a population of 263 in Edwardian times, turned out in force for Mr. Hindley and his camera. On the right of this view was once a shop and post office, but the village has no retail outlets now, just a pub in the shape of the 'Nevile Arms'. The Grantham Canal meanders its way around Kinoulton, providing very pleasant walks.

Cotgrave

The Village, Cotgrave, Notts.

A great gathering at Cotgrave for this picture on card no. 442, posted from the village to Sheffield in June 1911. The population of 659 in 1901 rose to over 7,000 during the century, largely because of the sinking of a pit in 1963 and an influx of miners and their families from the north-east. That shut in 1994, and though the population subsequently fell, a new housing estate east of the village has boosted it again. All Saints Church, whose origins lie in the 12th century, is in the picture here, with the village school on the left.

Stoke Ferry

Postcard no. 24. Two ferry boats, which used a rope pulley to cross the river, can be seen on the picture, with the nearer one carrying at least seven people, a dog, and a horse and cart. The 'Ferry Inn' on the north bank is still very popular. We reached the photo point by bicycle from the village of Shelford. Stoke Bardolph, the nearby village, had a population of 213 at the time the postcard was published.

'Clumber' postcard no. 84. These children have been released from the local school (behind the trees and houses) to appear in Albert Hindley's photo, a trick which helped to increase postcard sales. Down the hill is the 'Royal Oak'. Population of the village in 1906 was 756, while now it hovers around 1,800. It had two windmills, both now converted into private properties.

Gunthorpe

This card didn't find its way into the postal system until May 1944, when it was sent from Nottingham to Sheffield. This c.1906 view on the East Bridgford side of the river shows a scene with a sailboat and two working barges, while today the river here is often crowded with narrowboats and motor boats. The postcard is also found captioned 'East Bridgford'. Gunthorpe has a lively restaurant, pub and leisure activity buzz, with plenty to see at the nearby lock (off photo, to the left). The river has a weir now, with all craft funnelled through the lock, built by Nottingham Corporation in 1925. To the left of the postcard was a toll bridge (1873-1925). To the left of the photo, further upstream, is the road bridge that replaced it.

Hoveringham

Un-numbered postcard, The ferry here dates from the 17th century, when a house (right, demolished in the 1960s) was built for the ferryman. By the 1830s an inn had been established, originally called the 'Old Ferry House' and later the 'Old Elm Tree', once a highly successful hotel. It closed in 1988 and is now an apartment complex. On the other side of the river is the village of Kneeton, on top of a steep wooded cliff. Access from there to the point where we took the photograph involved a climb down a very steep rough track (formerly a reasonably paved road, Kneeton Hill, where once there was a pulley system enabling goods transported by ferry to be taken to the top), and a reverse journey up an equally steep climb that, thanks to someone's thoughtfulness, involved steps. Kneeton, devoid of shops and an excuse for anyone to walk anywhere, was totally deserted on the day we were there, except for one moving car and a couple of dogs which were seemingly ownerless. In 1906 Kneeton's population was 113 and Hoveringham's 311. The ferryman had an important role in Edwardian times.

Above: no. 138 in the 'Clumber' series, showing the ferryman waiting for customers.

Hazelford Ferry

The Ferry, Hazelford, Notts.

Hazelford Ferry was near the village of Bleasby, and adjoining the 'Star and Garter' pub on the postcard above. The building is now a residential home. Postcard no. 20, sent from Nottingham to Chesterfield in September 1918. We didn't cross the river to replicate this view (actually, it was probably taken from the ferry boat), but the photos right and below right give an idea of what the place looks like now. The ferry slipway (below) is still used by people launching small boats and powered dinghies, and nearby river moorings are busy.

Card no. 275, sent to Sherwood in October 1921. This view looks towards the main part of the village from the Hazelford Ferry end. The horse, cart and men have paused outside the 'Fisherman's Rest' public house, now long closed, leaving the 'Wagon and Horses' as the only pub in the village. The building is now called 'Fisherman's Cottage'. A century or so ago, 287 folk lived in Bleasby, and at least they had the facility of a railway station on the Nottingham to Lincoln line, with 10 stopping passenger trains a day (two on Sundays). Newark was just 16 minutes away and Nottingham half-an-hour. Today, there's still a service roughly every two hours.

Nottingham Canal, Lenton

Midland Bridge, Lenton, Nottingham.

The Nottingham Canal, en route to Beeston, passes under the old Midland Railway bridge near Petersham Street, Gregory Street and Castle Boulevard. This tranquil scene is still present today, though the fence on which the young lady is sitting has been turned into a higher, more forbidding steel barrier. The houses on the right have been replaced with more modern structures. Today the canal is well-used by narrow barges, motor boats and canoeists, while the towpath is busy with walkers and cyclists. The lovely willow trees have masked the view of the railway bridge somewhat. Postcard no. 180, posted at Nottingham in October 1907.

Cut Through Lane, Lenton

Cut-through Lane still exists as a route through Nottingham University, greatly enlarged for road traffic, from the North entrance to West Lodge on the Beeston road, though it has been diverted in several places from the Edwardian path. Originally it was an extension of Spring Close (now obliterated by the Queen's Medical Centre), crossing Sandy Lane (now Clifton Boulevard) as a direct route to Beeston before University Boulevard existed. It is very difficult to place this location exactly - there are no surviving landmarks to pinpoint it - but the likeliest place would seem to be where Cut-through Lane began, halfway between the QMC roundabout and the Dunkirk flyover - at one of the entrances to the University (below). On this postcard, as a lady chats to the resident in the garden of the house to left of picture, I'm not quite sure what to make of the couple on the right! 'Clumber' card no. 82. Three road signs for the lane remain, including one very near the QMC roundabout - but this is not on the original route. From the Beeston end, the lane's route remains pretty much the same as it was.

Gregory Street, Lenton

The 'White Hart' pub at Lenton dates back to the early 19th century, and on this site previously was a farmhouse that had been turned into Lenton Coffee House. By the side of this inn is the site of the old debtors'prison, known as Old Peveril Gaol. On this postcard, the photographer has persuaded lots of village children to pose for him. This is postcard no. 170.

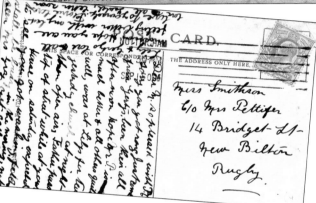

Busy traffic has replaced ambling sheep on Gregory Street. The postcard below is no.170, sent from Nottingham to Rugby in September 1909.

Park Gate, Lenton

The entrance to the Park Estate from Derby Road on postcard no. 256. To the right on the picture is the 'North Lodge Hotel'. The Park is a select residential development adjacent to Derby Road and Nottingham Castle. It includes two tennis clubs, one of which used to stage the prestigious Nottingham Open which attracted top players from all over the world. Access is restricted for non-residents. The term 'Lenton Sands', applied to the area at the top of Derby Road, derives its name from Sandy Field Common, itself probably so-called because of loose sand, imported by the monks at Lenton Priory, blew around the area.

The Cross, Beeston

THE CROSS, BEESTON, NOTTS.

Postcard no. 246, showing The Cross at Beeston, at the junctions of Grange Avenue, Dovecote Lane, Church Street and Middle Street. The building to the left is the Manor Lodge, and the chimney on the right is on the Manor House, possibly the oldest residence in the town. The photo below shows the main change to be the war memorial, erected after the Great War. Almost 9,000 people lived in Beeston at the start of the 20th century, most working on the iron foundry, cycle works, or lace and hosiery industries.

Main Road, Bramcote

This is now the unbelievably busy A52 (Brian Clough Way), with the current complex roundabout just over the brow of the hill. On the left is Church Street and on the right, today, is the entrance to Bramcote Leisure Centre and Bramcote Hills Park. On the right of the postcard is one of the pair of lodge houses at the entrance to Bramcote Hills House. Card no. 198, posted at Nottingham and addressed locally in February 1908. Bramcote was quite a large village in Edwardian days with 745 inhabitants. The photo below should have been taken from the middle of the road, but it seemed too dangerous to do that!

Attenborough Church

Card no. 37. This is not the most inspiring of comparative views in the book - there weren't even any cows! Attenborough, where Oliver Cromwell's son-in-law Henry Ireton lived, is now most famous for its nature reserve, developed from old quarries. St. Mary Magdalene's Church with its large early perpendicular type steeple dates from the 13th century.

Trent Railway Station

Trent railway station near Long Eaton, seen on postcard no. 218, was opened in 1862 and was once a busy junction, serving trains to London, Derby, Sheffield and Nottingham. But as far as passengers were concerned, it wasn't really that close to any communities, and was purely an interchange station. Travellers from Nottingham and Derby could join the London and Scotland trains. Anyway, it closed on New Year's Day 1968 and nothing of the station now remains, though trains rattle through to the same destinations they did in 1906. Taking a photograph was a challenge; getting anywhere near on foot was unrealistic, as Network Rail have sensibly restricted access, so the photos here were taken out of a train carriage window.

The site is now unrecognisable as a station, as seen above, but to put the location into context I've added views looking over to Ratcliffe-on-Soar Power Station, towards Trent Lock, and one of East Midlands Parkway station, the next one up the line (albeit over the border), dwarfed by the cooling towers.

Trent Lock

TRENT LOCK.

One of the later postcards, no. 633, featuring Trent Lock. It was posted from Long Eaton to Riseley, Bedfordshire, in August 1908. This is a delightful place on the River Trent where the River Soar and the Erewash Canal flow in. It is on the border of Leicestershire, Derbyshire and Nottinghamshire; Ratcliffe-on-Soar Power Station is dominant nearby and the Midland Main line track runs nearby into East Midlands Parkway railway station. With planes coming in to land at the nearby East Midlands Airport, this is a place to relax and take in the atmosphere - and there are plenty of good eateries here, too. On the right of the photo are the 'Steamboat' restaurant and the 'Lock House Tea Rooms', while the 'Trent Lock' pub is nearby.

Derby Road, Long Eaton

DERBY ROAD. LONG EATON.

Ok, technically Long Eaton is in Derbyshire, being just on the western side of the River Erewash, but it has a Nottingham postcode and it was high on the list of Albert Hindley's postcard priorities, so we thought we'd stretch a point and give it an honorary inclusion. This is 'Clumber' card no. 646. Replicating this scene involved waiting for a set of pedestrian lights to stop the traffic on the left of the road so I could jump out into the middle and take the photo. The contrast encapsulates everything that has happened to our streets in the past century. On the left is the spire of the old Bethel Methodist Church, opened in 1904 and closed as a place of worship in 1980. It is now the Oasis Christian Centre. In the centre distance is the Christ Church Methodist building.

Postcard no. 438. When these houses were built, they were in a prime position on the then quiet road out of town towards Nottingham. Now they are on a very busy thoroughfare. At the time of publication of this and the previous postcard, Long Eaton's population was just over 13,000 and lace-making (at its peak during the Edwardian era) and a railway carriage works were the principal sources of employment.

Derby Road, Stapleford

Derby Rᵈ. Stapleford, Notts.

This is now a very busy road at the centre of Stapleford, portayed here in a quieter mode on 'Clumber' card no. 200, posted at Stapleford in May 1912 and sent to a Sheffield address. Stapleford's population at the time was almost 6,000, and was a centre of lace and silk manufacturing. The two shops on the right are Bell & Co., chemist and druggist, and the Globe Tea Co.

Derby & Nottingham Road, Stapleford

The photographer has just turned round from his stance for the previous card to take this picture for a postcard. The 'Old Rock' pub (the white building in the photo below) is a survivor from card no. 434, though until December 2016 it was called 'The Chequers'. On the immediate left are the premises of the Globe Tea Company (it featured on both these cards!), but the Primitive Methodist Chapel further along was demolished to make way for shops and offices in 1973. As elsewhere, heavy traffic, now controlled by lights, is constant.

Cottages, Clifton

Cottages, Clifton, Nottingham.

For some reason, Albert Hindley selected this view for the second postcard in the 'Clumber' series. This one was posted at Nottingham in May 1906, addressed to Sheffield. Tracing this view took a while, and only one of the two thatched cottages remains. Clifton Village is a quiet backwater separated from, but dwarfed by, the post-war development on the far side of the main road that everyone thinks of as Clifton. Pre-First World War the village was called Clifton-with-Glapton, having a population of 362.

Four Lane Ends, Clifton

FOUR LANE ENDS, CLIFTON, NOTTS.

Sent from Nottingham to a local address, this is no. 29 in the series. Behind the cameraman is the imposingly large dovecote on the village green which is still there. As with Oxton's Three Lane Ends, no-one seems to use the phrase in this postcard caption any more. We struggled with this one, and trust that the location - just by what is now the busy A453 road - is the right choice.

Clifton Grove Farm

CLIFTON GROVE FARM NOTTS.

Postcard no. 32 in the 'Clumber' series, posted at Nottingham to a local address in November 1905. Grove Farm was near what is now the Clifton road bridge over the Trent. The Prince of Wales (future Edward VIII) bought it in 1927, to facilitate an affair with a local girl, the daughter of a landowner who lived at Lamcote House near Radcliffe-on-Trent, and sold it when the romance cooled in 1933. The farm then passed through various hands before being acquired by Nottingham University in 1960. They used the land for sports fields. The farmhouse building is still standing, and the scene viewed from the other side of the river (accessed via a short walk from the 'Harvester' restaurant on Wilford Lane) is pretty similar.

Clifton Hall

Getting a decent photo of this building today from the same location that Albert Hindley used for 'Clumber' card no. 320 was tough. Clifton Hall is adjacent to Clifton St. Mary's Church, and it was from the grounds of the latter that we took two photos that as a composite form the one below. Taking a picture from the same spot as on the above would have meant the Hall being almost totally obscured by trees! Clifton Hall has had an exciting history from its development by the De Clifton family in the late 13th century. The family's involvement with national politics and key events (Sir Gervase Clifton was beheaded after the Battle of Tewkesbury in 1471) would make a book on its own. They held the place until the mid-20th century, remodelling it c.1780 in a Georgian style. In 1958 the hall became the Clifton Hall Girls' Grammar School, before Trent Polytechnic (later Nottingham Trent University) took it over from 1976 to 2002. Since then it has been privately-owned, with one owner having an application to hold civil weddings turned down. He then quit, claiming the Hall was haunted. Rumours of paranormal activity had surfaced occasionally since the Hall was a school.

Gotham Church & Pump

Card no. 48. Just over a thousand people lived in Gotham at the start of the 20th century, while now it is around 1,560. The village gained a perhaps unwanted fame in the tale of the 'wise men of Gotham', from the villagers who pretended to be mad to avoid having to pay for a highway in the reign of King John. As a result, Gotham may well have been the inspiration for Gotham City in the *Batman* stories. St. Lawrence's Church has a remarkable 13th century steeple, rebuilt in the late 1700s, when the chancel and aisles were also renovated. The striking arched entrance to the burial ground seen on the postcard is no longer there.

Nottingham Road, Gotham

Nottingham Rd. Gotham, Notts.

"This is where you got arf & arf on the road coming from Barton", wrote someone on the back of this unposted postcard, no. 304 in the 'Clumber' series. Whatever that means, it wouldn't happen now - the road to Barton is no longer a thoroughfare, cut off by the rejuvenated A453. The 'Star Inn' is still here, but the area has been changed radically.

The Pump, Gotham

Another view of the Pump at Gotham, with the 'Sun Inn' behind it. This pub, which dates from the 1840s, was originally three cottages which were knocked into one. The facade has since been freshened up. Postcard no. 505 in the series.

The Ferry, Thrumpton

THE FERRY, THRUMPTON.

The buildings on the north bank of the River Trent at Thrumpton were the plaster works of the Trent Mining Company. The entire complex has now been demolished, and the last ferry, run by the Priestley family, crossed in 1968. This is another of the 'Clumber' cards with a large border, no. 632. Recorded population of Thrumpton in 1906 was 167, and the latest 2011 census revealed it as just two fewer. Thrumpton Hall (on the postcard below, no. 283, sent from Long Eaton to Haverhill in 1908), a popular event venue, is the main feature of the village. The photo is taken from a different angle to show the ferry slipways on both banks.

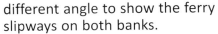

THRUMPTON HALL, NOTTS

Barton-in-Fabis Village

Barton-in-Fabis, formerly known as Barton-in-the-Beans, has a population now of around 250, which has remained fairly stable for over a century. Despite its small size and distance from Nottingham, Albert Hindley deemed it worthy of five postcards, more than the larger and closer Keyworth and Plumtree, for instance. The village Post Office, now a private house, is on the right of the postcard top left (no. 115 in the series), midway down the street. Below is no. 116.

Barton is on the opposite side of the River Trent from Attenborough, and a ferry used to operate across it. In 1906 the ferry was a large steam-powered vessel. It was a half-mile walk from the village to reach the river bank, though!

The 'Clumber' series of picture postcards, published 1904-1912

1 Nottingham, Arboretum
2 Clifton, cottages
3 Nottingham, Mansfield Road
4 Sherwood, Mansfield Road
5 Sherwood railway tunnel
6 Sherwood railway station
6 Nottingham Castle
7 Daybrook, church
8 Nottingham, Market Place
9 Colwick Road & wood
10 Gedling, Main Street
11 Carlton, railway crossing
12 Colwick railway station
13 Colwick Vale
14 Colwick Weir
15 Colwick, cow drinks
16 Colwick lock
17 Radcliffe-on-Trent, Manvers Arms
18 Radcliffe-on-Trent, church
19 Radcliffe-on-Trent, cliffs
19 Red Hill
20 Hazelford Ferry
21 Hoveringham Ferry
22 Nottingham Arboretum bandstand
23 Gunthorpe bridge
24 Stoke ferry
25 Holme Pierrpoint lock
26 West Bridgford, Lady Bay
27 West Bridgford, church
28 Nottingham, General Hospital
29 Clifton, Four Lane Ends
30 Clifton, entrance to Grove
31 Clifton Grove
32 Clifton, Grove Farm
33 Colwick, trees on Trent
34 Nottingham Castle
35 Nuthall
36 Nottingham High School
37 Attenborough, church
38 Beeston, Mitchell's boathouse
39 Beeston, church
40 Beeston locks
41 Trent College
42 Long Eaton, Derby Road
43 Long Eaton, Sawley Road
43 Arnold, Notingham Road
44 Thrumpton ferry
45 Chilwell
46 Hemlock Stone
47 Hucknall Torkard, market
47 Nottingham Castle, new gateway
48 Gotham, church & pump
49 Lenton, boatyard
50 Lenton, Gregory Street bridge
51 Kimberley, Trinity Church
51 Nottingham Arboretum, flower beds
52 Nuthall, church
53 Gamston Lane
54 Gamston village
55 Ruddington, church
56 Ruddington, Main Road
57 Nottingham, School of Art
57 Bulwell Hall flower garden
58 Kimberley cemetery
58 Nottingham Arboretum, rustic bridge
59 East Leake, church
60 Welbeck Abbey
61 Costock
62 Barton, old cottages
63 Nottingham Castle + heraldic crest
64 Nottingham Market Place + crest
65 Trent Bridge + crest
66 Wollaton hall + crest
67 Wilford, cottages + crest
68 Colwick Hall + crest
69 Nottingham, St. Peter's Church
70 Nottingham, Children's Hospital
71 West Bridgford, Musters Road
72 Wilford, cow drinks
73 Arnold, church
74 Burton Joyce, church
74 Nottingham, King Edward Park

75 Burton Joyce, sheep
76 Burton Joyce, cows
77 Wilford, cottages
78 Wilford, church
79 Bestwood Lodge
80 Bestwood Lodge, entrance
81 Daybrook cemetery
82 Lenton, Cut-through Lane
82a Lenton, Cut-through Lane (different view)

Another postcard - no. 82a - of Cut-through Lane, Lenton

83 East Bridgford, windmill
84 East Bridgford, children
85 East Bridgford, church
86 Gunthorpe Hall
87 Colwick Racecourse
88 Colwick Hall
89 Nottingham, church cemetery
89 Kinoulton
90 Clifton, church
91 Nottingham, Walter Fountain
92 Nottingham, Forest top walk
93 Nottingham, Theatre & Empire
94 Nottingham, Vernon Park
95 Attenborough, ferry
96 Nottingham, St. Mary's Church
97 Nottingham, Castle & steps
98 Nottingham, Forest Road
99 Belvoir Castle
99 Carlton, library & fire station
100 Wollaton, canal bridge
101 Dunkirk, Abbey Street bridge
102 Nottingham, Queen Victoria statue
103 Wilford, Trentside
104 Bulcote
105 Nottingham, Castle Ravine
106 Nottingham, the Forest
107 Nottingham, Elm Avenue
108 Nottingham Arboretum, the Aviary
109 Wollaton, church
110 Holme Pierrepont Hall & church
111 Bottesford, church
112 Bottesford, whipping post & stocks
113 Barton-in-Fabis, church
114 Barton-in-Fabis
115 Barton village
116 Barton-in-Fabis
117 Bingham, Market Place
118 Bingham, church
119 Bingham, rectory
120 Stapleford, ye old cross
121 Lambley, church
122 Wilford Bridge
123 Bunny, church
124 Daybrook railway station
125 Daybrook
126 Old Colwick, church
127 Nottingham, Market Place
128 Nottingham, St. Andrew's Church
129 Nottingham, St. Mary's Church porch

130 Long Eaton, Wesleyan church
131 Nottingham, Mansfield Road
132 Nottingham, Mansfield Road
133 Nottingham, Castle gateway & drill hall
134 Nottingham, Milton Street
135 Nottingham, Postern Gate
136 Thrumpton Hall lodge
137 Long Eaton, Lime Grove
137 Nottingham, Park Steps
138 Nottingham, Queen's Walk
138 Hoveringham Ferry
139 Nottingham, Long Row
140 Nottingham, Forest entrance
141 Nottingham, Carrington church
142 Nottingham, Bobbers' Mill
143 Nottingham, Narrow Marsh
144 Nottingham, The Poultry
145 Nottingham, Kirke White's birthplace
146 Nottingham, Holy Trinity Church
147 Nottingham, Woodborough Road
148 Nottingham, Arboretum
149 Mapperley, tram terminus
150 Nottingham, Bluecoat schools
151 Sherwood, tram sheds
152 Nottingham, Mansfield Road, Wesleyan chapel
152 Nottingham, Mansfield Road
153 Bulwell golf links
154 Bulwell, Market Place
155 Bulwell, tram terminus
156 Bulwell, church
157 Bulwell golf links, ladies' pavilion
158 Nottingham, Sneinton baths
159 Nottingham, Castle entrance
160 Nottingham, Derby Road, cemetery entrance
161 Bunny Hall Lodge
162 Nottingham, general cemetery
163 Nottingham, Grand Theatre
164 Nottingham, Victoria Park
165 Sneinton, Southwell Road
166 Sneinton Market
167 Nottingham, Alexandra Park
168 Basford railway crossing
168 Nottingham, The Exchange
169 Lenton, Priory church
170 Lenton, Gregory Street
171 Nottingham, Bentinck Road corner
172 Lambley Lane
173 Lambley Lane from Crow Park
174 Burton Joyce railway station
175 Burton Joyce
176 Burton Joyce from Crow Park
177 Bulcote, church
178 Lowdham, church
179 Lowdham, railway station approach
180 Lowdham, railway station

Lowdham railway station, still open today. No. 180 in the 'Clumber' series. This postcard was sent to an address in Sneinton in July 1908.

180 Lenton, Midland bridge
181 Lenton village
181 Lowdham village
182 Nottingham, Albert Hall
183 Nottingham, Castlegate Congregational church
184 Nottingham, All Saints Church

185 Long Eaton, Primitive Methodist church
186 Beeston, Wesleyan church
187 Nottingham, Castle grounds
188 Wollaton Park Road
189 Wollaton, old cottage
190 Wollaton, balloon houses
191 Sandiacre, church
192 Sandiacre, Post Office Square
192 Trent Bridge, Lovers' walk
193 Bramcote, old church
194 Stapleford, Risley Brook
195 Stapleford, library & fire station
196 Stapleford, Lovers' walk
197 Stapleford cemetery
198 Stapleford, Derby Road
198a Bramcote, Main Road
199 Long Eaton cemetery
200 Long Eaton railway station

Long Eaton railway station, still open today. Card no.200, sent to Bexleyheath in March 1907

200 Stapleford, Derby Road
201 Long Eaton Parish Church
202 Long Eaton, Derby Road
203 Old Basford, St. Leodegarius's Church
204 Edwalton, church
205 Nottingham, Tennyson Street Wesleyan Chapel
206 Bulwell, new golf pavilion
207 Whatton-in-the-Vale village
208 Whatton-in-the-Vale
209 Whatton-in-the-Vale church
210 Old Colwick village
211 Colwick Woods & cricket ground
212 Colwick railway crossing
213 Netherfield, Wesleyan Church
214 Netherfield, church
215 Gedling
216 Gedling, church
217 Trent Bridge cricket ground
218 Trent railway station
219 Aslockton, church
220 Cotgrave, church
221 Nottingham, Mundella Council Schools
222 Nottingham, colours of 59th 2nd Notts Regiment in St. Mary's Church
223 Nottingham, St. Mary's Church interior
224 Nottingham, Gordon Memorial Home
224 Hucknall Torkard, High Street & church
225 Nottingham, St. Philip's Church

St. Philip's Church, Sneinton (no. 225), exists no longer.

226 Sneinton, St. Stephen's church
227 Wilford, the Round House
228 Wilford, Kirke White's Cottage
229 Nottingham, Addison Street bridge over Arboretum
230 Nottingham, Robin Hood's Caves, Church cemetery

231 Nottingham, Hyson Green Boulevard
232 Nottingham, Forest Road & cemetery lodge
233 Mapperley, St. Jude's Church
234 Nottingham, St. James's Church
235 Cropwell Bishop, church
236 Cropwell Bishop, Nottingham Road
237 Cropwell Bishop, Main Road
238 Cropwell Butler, Radcliffe Road
239 Nottingham, University College Entrance
240 Radcliffe, ferry & boathouse
241 Edwalton, Melton Road
242 Tollerton Hall
243 Tollerton Hall Lodge
244 Tollerton Hall, church
245 Nottingham, Robin Hood's Chase
246 Beeston, the Cross
247 Nottingham, the Park, Lenton Road
248 Oxton
249 Oxton, Three Lane Ends
250 Oxton, church
251 Calverton, church
252 Arnold, Main Street
253 Arnold, Ebenezer Chapel
254 Nottingham, Mansfield Road Grosvenor Corner
255 Nottingham, Redcliffe Road church
256 Nottingham, Park Gate, Lenton Sands
257 Nottingham, new suspension bridge
257 Nottingham, Queen's Walk
258 Nottingham, new suspension bridge
259 West Bridgford, Trent Boulevard
260 West Bridgford, Wesleyan church
261 West Bridgford, Musters Road
262 Lenton, church
263 Epperstone
264 Hucknall Torkard, Zachariah Green's house
265 Hucknall Torkard, church & Market Place
266 Nottingham, Old Radford church
267 Victoria Embankment approach
268 Nottingham Midland railway station interior
269 Nottingham, the Lace Market
270 Nottingham, St. Ann's Well
271 Nottingham, St. Ann's church
272 Basford cemetery
273 Thurgarton, church
274 Bleasby, church
275 Bleasby village
276 West Bridgford, Radcliffe Road
277 West Bridgford, canal & Lady Bay bridge
278 Bestwood Ironworks
279 Bestwood Parish Church & schools
280 Arnold, Red Hill
281 Trent Lodge, RHR Range
282 Willoughby-on-the-Wolds church
283 Thrumpton Hall
284 Thrumpton, church
285 Thrumpton post office
286 Moorgreen, The Mansion, High Park Wood
287 Moorgreen, Felley Riding, High Park Wood
288 Greasley, church
288 Wilford, church
289 Eastwood, Ivy Lane
290 Eastwood Hall
290 Wilford, embankment & railway bridge
291 Eastwood Rectory
291 Wilford Bridge entrance
292 Eastwood cemetery
292 Trent Embankment entrance
293 Langley Mill, River Erewash
294 Langley Mill, mill lock
295 Langley Mill, mills
296 Langley Mill, Cocker House
296 Sneinton Hollows
297 Langley Mill, Aldecar Hall
297 Nottingham, Hippodrome
298 Eastwood, Derby Road
298 Trent Bridge
299 Strelley, Broad Oak
300 Strelley, church
301 Bradmore, Main Road
302 Bilborough, church

303 Langley Mill, Aldecar church
303 Lenton, church
304 Eastwood, canal
304 Gotham, Nottingham Road
305 Arnold, Parish Church
306 Arnold, Carnegie Library
307 Nottingham, Corporation Oaks
308 Bradmore
309 West Bridgford, post office
310 West Bridgford Hall
311 West Bridgford, rectory
312 West Bridgford, Hall lodge
313 Carlton, Carnegie Library
314 Linby, Market Cross & maypole
315 Linby, church
316 Papplewick, the dam
317 Papplewick

Papplewick features as no. 317 in the series

318 Annesley Hall Lodge
319 Annesley Cemetery
320 Clifton Hall
321 Nottingham Arboretum, Chinese Bell
321 Sneinton, General Booth's birthplace
322 Clifton village
323 Colwick, eel fishing
324 Heanor, church
324 Bulwell Hall
325 Eastwood, Parish Church
325 Bulwell Hall, the lodge

The Lodge Gates for the now-demolished Bulwell Hall. Card no. 325, posted at Nottingham in August 1909 and sent to Ipswich

326 Sawley, Trent Bridge & Old Toll House
327 Sawley canal bridge
328 Sawley, church
329 Gedling
330 Nottingham, Mundella Schools
331 Nottingham, General Booth's birthplace
332 Keyworth, church
333 Keyworth, Hawthorn Cottage
334 Keyworth, Bunny Lane
335 Plumtree, Main Road
336 Nottingham, Clumber Street
337 Sneinton Boulevard
338 Hyson Green, St. Stephen's Church
339 Nottingham, Wollaton Park gates
340 Wilford, Ruddington Road
341 Plumtree, church
342 Plumtree, Keyworth Road
343 Radcliffe-on-Trent village
344 Ruddington, Church Street
345 Nottingham, King Street
346 Nottingham, Congregational College
347 Nottingham Castle
348 Nottingham Arboretum, rustic bridge
349 Nottingham Arboretum
350 Nottingham, Broad Street Wesleyan Chapel

351 Nottingham, Victoria station & hotel
352 Trent Bridge, landing stage
352 Carlton Church
353 Nottingham, Free Library
354 Wilford, cottages, Ruddington Road
355 Trent Bridge embankment
355 Barton-in-Fabis
356 Trent Bridge, children's holiday
357 Nottingham, Long Row Market
358 Nottingham, market
359 Nottingham post office
360 The Trent, steamer & boat houses
361 Shelford, church
362 Hoveringham, the mills
363 Nottingham, Colwick Road
364 Nottingham Market, market day
365 Woodborough church
366 Woodborough, Main Street
367 Nottingham, The Forest, parade ground
368 Nottingham, The Forest from Bentinck Road
369 Nottingham Arboretum, Waverley Street
370 Nottingham, Arboretum lodge
371 Daybrook, Mansfield Road
372 Daybrook, cottages
373 Nottingham, castle gates
374 Nottingham, Mechanics' Hall
375 Cossall, church
376 Costock, Red Lion Hotel
377 Costock, the village
377 Woodthorpe Drive, Notts
379 Costock, old mill
381 Mapperley Plains
382 Mapperley, Westdale Lane
384 Nottingham, Colwick Road, The Roundhouse
385 Carlton, Burton Road
387 Kimberley, Digby Colliery
388 Granby village

The Erewash, Stapleford. Card no. 433

Carnegie Library, Long Eaton, no. 645, posted from there to Newark in May 1912.

442 Cotgrave village
447 Nottingham, Trent Bridge (oval frame)
449 River Trent (multiview)
450 Wilford (multiview)
451 Nottingham Castle (multiview)
463 West Bridgford, Masonic Hall
478 Hoveringham, Kneeton Hall
504 Gotham, Little London
505 Gotham, the pump
506 Gotham village
507 Gotham, church
602 Belvoir Castle
604 Nottingham, new suspension bridge
605 Calverton, Woodborough Road
608 Beeston, the Trent
611 Nottingham, church cemetery
619 Nottingham, Goose Fair
620 Calverton, Main Street
621 Ruddington, Manor House
622 Calverton Hall
632 Nottingham, Hippodrome
632 Thrumpton, the ferry
633 Trent Lock
635 Nottingham, General Hospital from Castle grounds

638 Hucknall Torkard, church
644 Long Eaton, church
645 Long Eaton, Carnegie Library
646 Long Eaton, Derby Road
651 Thrumpton Hall lodge
658 Cotgrave Place

Un-numbered postcards
Beeston, the Trent
Colwick Hall & crest
Daybrook church
Gedling railway station
Gunthorpe
Hoveringham
Lady Bay
Major Oak, Dukeries
Nottingham Castle + crest
Nuthall Temple
Ruddington
Ruddington, South Manor
Trent Bridge, landing stage + crest

Granby Village, no. 388

392 Wilford
393 Daybrook Vale
394 Arnold, Front Street
395 Arnold, Thackeray's Lane
396 Arno Vale, Notts
397 Carlton, Burton Road
398 Sherwood, Edwards Lane
398 Colwick, railway crossing
400 Nottingham, Goose Fair

Goose Fair (in the Market Place), no. 400

401 Nottingham, Goose Fair
402 Newstead Abbey
433 Stapleford, The Erewash
434 Stapleford, Derby & Nottingham Roads
435 Stapleford, The Hall
436 Toton
438 Long Eaton, Nottingham Road

Other Nottinghamshire books from Reflections of a Bygone Age

We also publish a range of 'Yesterday's Nottinghamshire' books in A5 size with 40 pages, priced between £3.50 and £4.95.

1. Nottinghamshire Inns & Pubs
2. West Bridgford
3. Keyworth
4. Nottinghamshire Cricketers
5. Beeston
6. Nottinghamshire Railway Stations
7. Ruddington
8. Regiments of Nottinghamshire*
9. Nottinghamshire Trams*
10. River Trent
11. Retford
12. Cigarette Cards of Nottinghamshire
13. Radcliffe-on-Trent
14. Arnold vol 1
15. Bingham*
16. Newark
17. Nottingham's Lost Landmarks
18. Southwell*
19. Arnold vol 2*
20. Carlton, Netherfield & Colwick*
21. Worksop
22. Bulwell
23. The Dukeries*
24. Eastwood
25. Sutton-in-Ashfield*
26. Hucknall
27. Wollaton
28. Radford, Hyson Green & The Forest

29. The Meadows in the 1970s
30. Mapperley & Sherwood*
31. Nottinghamshire Inns & Pubs vol 2
32. Lenton & The Park*
33. Sneinton & St. Ann's
34. Stapleford & Bramcote
35. Burton Joyce
36. Lowdham, Lambley & Gonalston
37. Boots the Chemists
38. A Village Tour - Hoveringham, Bleasby & area
39. Nottinghamshire Collieries
40. Nottingham City Centre
41. Kirkby-in-Ashfield
42. Nottinghamshire Steam Railways in the 1960s
43. Nottingham Forest Football Club
44. Notts County Football Club
45. Nottinghamshire Post Offices
46. Goose Fair
47. Nottingham Castle
48. Mansfield
49. Robin Hood
50. Nottingham Events & Disasters
51. Nottinghamshire Steam Railways in the 1960s vol 2
52. Beeston vol two

* currently out of print

We also publish similar volumes for other counties. Please ring 0115 937 4079 for full list, or check our website www.postcardcollecting.co.uk

About the writer, photographer and researcher

Brian Lund and his wife **Mary** founded publishing company Reflections of a Bygone Age in 1980 and have published over 200 books, mostly based on old picture postcard images, on different areas of England and on subjects such as Golf, Cricket, Railways, Mining and Pubs. 52 of those books are in the 'Yesterday's Nottinghamshire' series. They also edited and published a monthly magazine for postcard collectors for 35 years, as well as a special Annual edition, and introduced two other collectors' magazines. Reflections have also published many contemporary local picture postcards. Brian played rugby and cricket in both his native Yorkshire and here in Nottinghamshire for many years, while Mary has majored on tennis, hockey, golf and squash. Despite his Yorkshire heritage, Brian is an enthusiastic promoter of Nottingham, and collaborated with Rob and music producer Richard Williams on three music videos featuring Nottingham songs (available by googling 'brian and rich youtube').

For the photos he contributed to the book, Brian used a Nikon DX camera.

Mary accompanied him on most of those photoshoots where they left Rob at home, and acted as chauffeur, researcher and location-finder.

Rob Inglis is a professional photographer. Having retired from a full frontline police service role, he turned his hobby into a profession, qualifying with a foundation degree and started on a new journey into wedding, commercial and event photography. He became the vice-chair of a local camera club and enjoys taking images for competitions when time allows.

Brian and Rob are close friends, having been at school together. They also shared a passion for playing rugby. Rob says: *"Brian's Edwardian project appealed to me and I had to be involved. It embraced detective work, and using my knowledge of Nottingham to capture images from the same spot that someone had chosen to stand in some 114 years ago! It was amazing that local people we spoke to had such a historical knowledge of their local area and some scenes almost matched identically those of history yet others were non-existent.*

My favourite comparison is the entrance to the Victoria Embankment as the same trees show their maturity over the years.

For the project I used Nikon's benchmark D850 which is a full frame 45.7 mega pixel digital SLR camera with a Nikon f2.8 ED 24-70mm lens to give scope for matching the framing of the original postcards. We decided early spring would be the best time as the trees would not be in full leaf and therefore not restrict any vistas. I used a technique of HDR photography to which I took three different exposures of the same scene to give an under-exposed, an over-exposed and a correctly exposed image. By combining these in Adobe Lightroom and Photoshop it enables more detail to be visible in the shadow and light areas".